1

In Dogs We Trust

"To love at all is to be vulnerable. Love anything, and your heart will certainly be wrung and possibly broken. If you want to make sure of keeping it intact, you must give your heart to no one, not even to an animal. Wrap it carefully round with hobbies and little luxuries; avoid all entanglements; lock it up safe in the casket or coffin of your selfishness. But in that casket, safe, dark, motionless, airless, it will change. It will not be broken; it will become unbreakable, impenetrable, irredeemable." - C.S. Lewis

Every dog is special. They are referred to as Angels. Bodhisattvas, Heavenly Messengers.... All meant to teach us patience, compassion and unconditional love. At times when any human would abandon us, they provide the comfort and emotional refuge we need to collect ourselves and become whole and productive again. They act as a conduit to all things spiritual and healing.

A year ago I knew I needed a divine mediator. The world had become increasingly terrifying. I had seen and experienced unspeakable evil. I learned firsthand that there truly is nothing one man will not do to another. I endured betrayal, and near death tortures that should have taken my life. I needed a companion more compassionate than the ever-present thoughts of suicide that were beginning to feel like friends. I survived the ordeals by reaching out to those in worse circumstances than myself. That has not stopped and this book is a testament to that drive. I have not always gotten it right, nor have I had the emotional and physical wherewithal to properly defend myself, but I have never let those near me be exploited if I could help it.

Gander, whose pictures populate this book, was an answer to prayers. He and my loving, long-suffering wife have restored me to some semblance of sanity.

Gander, and his uncanny ability to vanquish emotional resistance and social fear, has brought dozens of people and their stories into my life. Had it not been for Gander the counselor, teacher, ambassador, therapist, healer (and just dog), for hundreds of people that we met this year, this book would not exist.

Gander's page on Facebook has become one of the most positive places I visit on the Internet. He brings a smile to a lot of faces daily. He is the catalyst for information exchange and caring in a giving community wherein people can fetch ideas to effect change in their lives, celebrate their own spectacular relationship with a pet, or ask for help to improve the quality of their lives. The page has connected dozens of people with information needed to find their own service dogs and it has helped educate thousands about the need for canine co-therapists in physical and emotional struggles.

I have, through Gander, come to realize what an enormous need exists for more service dogs. I have learned that hundreds of victims of trauma (PTSD, sexual...) feel that they would have killed themselves long ago had a service dog not been part of their lives. Twenty-one veterans kill themselves daily. Had a Gander been in their lives the outcome could have been different.

Gander is the reason this book exists. The telling of his story as a rescue, and his rescue of me, has put me in touch with dozens of talented writers who share some incredible tales here. They all, many of them NYT best-selling authors, donated their work to this project.

This anthology's purpose is to share tales of inspiration, humor and devotion while raising funds for agencies who save lives: Rescue, Veteran and Service Dog charities will receive 100% of the profit generated by this book. We have chosen a mill dog charity, a veterans retreat, a 25-year old service dog agency that gives half of its dogs to wounded warriors and the other half to civilians with disabilities and a service dog education and assistance group, a Warrior Dog group, and a scholarship fund started by the family of fallen Medal of Honor Winner, Lt. Michael Murphy.

Gander and I will be traveling as time and health allow this year to educate and inform about service dogs as we pay tribute to fallen warriors who took their own lives. They too are casualties of war. We will also be collecting stories for a new book about the fallen that we will call Fetch.

Doctors, Psychologists, Nurses, Actors, Former SEALs, Housewives, Active Duty Warriors and people from all walks of life have contributed to this anthology, and I hope and believe we will improve the health and wellbeing of others in having done so. Your purchase of this book and your spreading the word too may well be instrumental in bringing peace to a trauma survivor, a wounded warrior or save a dog, like Gander, possibly facing execution.

Thank you for being part of our journey. Thank you for funding what I know to be an important mission. Enjoy some spectacular writing and thank you for helping spread the word about this book.

LB "Veteran Traveler" Hodge and Gander, SD

Dedication

This book is dedicated to those suffering with invisible wounds and to the twenty-one soldiers who daily take their own lives.

Table of Contents

Foreword

by Alex Thurman

As the editor of In Dogs We Trust, I have a shocking confession to make: I'm not really, or at least until recently haven't been, much of a "dog person."

Oh, I've never disliked dogs, except perhaps for two ferocious tiny (Chihuahuas? Pomeranians? Small dog owners, don't bite my head off!), encountered at a friend's house several years ago, whose bravura display of raw temperament, yapping domination, and lack of respect for my bodily space have been the subject of my nightmares ever since. Also, I'll admit, I've been afraid of a few big dogs. You know the kind: dogs wearing spiked collars, standing with their front legs akimbo by the sides of even scarier looking men in dark leather with flat, cold eyes? Those dogs.

But mostly I've enjoyed dogs. I've enjoyed watching large canines lollop across lawns with their tongues and tails flapping in the breeze. I've smiled at small dogs trotting proudly by the sides of the people they own, their short legs tapping out a brisk, determined rhythm on the side of the road. Dogs in all their stubborn, comical, heartbreaking particularity: in the abstract, I've been appreciative. But I'd never felt the urge to "have" a dog. Never imagined following an undoubtedly labor-intensive furry person down the sidewalk several times each day with a scoop and plastic bag in hand. I'd certainly never imagined giving my heart to one.

Then I met Gander, a large, brown, bearded Labradoodle Bodhisattva. Gander, who taught me, in one of those instant and indescribable ways that only angels or Buddha's can, that the world is far more miraculous than the grasping human mind can understand. Years ago, in a time and place far, far away, I'd gotten to know Lon Hodge, a remarkably gifted writer, therapist, Vietnam Vet, social agitator, traveler, raconteur, and visionary. But then we lost touch, for too long, as busy people often do. When I caught up with Lon again, I hardly recognized in the quiet, subdued man I saw the once preternaturally vital agitator for social good and plain general liveliness I'd once known.

The years since we'd met had brought some hard things into Lon's life. With those hard things, other things long suppressed, his service during and after Vietnam, childhood abuse, the loss of his father to wounds from his own time in Vietnam (yes, Lon is a Veteran son of a Veteran, proud in his tradition of generational service) surfaced, haunting his days and his nights until he was a broken shadow of himself.

Dangerous, though legal drugs, benign neglect, an overburdened healthcare system: like so many other Vets before and after him, the remedies offered by the system in place hadn't helped Lon on his path to recovery much at all.

But then a year ago, still enough the warrior to push for the care he and others who have served richly deserve, Lon arranged to be gifted with a service dog who could help him navigate his way back into the world. Gander had been, himself, one of the world's undeserved throwaways. His full story is a story only Lon deserves to tell. Suffice it to say that when, after instruction by prisoners at a Colorado women's prison (whose own salvation took the form of helping lost dogs become boon companions), and further training from Freedom Service Dogs, Gander met Lon Hodge, it was a meeting of two great, wounded souls.

When I had the privilege of getting together with Lon for dinner one evening not long after they came together, Gander was by his side. Upon meeting him I knew in an instant that my life was also about to be changed. I knew it, if for no other reason, because in the few short weeks since Gander and Lon had pledged themselves to one another as lifetime companions, the man I'd once known had returned, ready and able to take on the world again. Not an instant cure, but an unmistakable healing. I saw it in both of them, and I've seen it grow ever since.

So when Lon, and (alright I'll say it!) Gander asked me to edit a book about the bond between humans and dogs, all the proceeds of which would go to helping prevent the growing scourge of suicide among military Vets, what answer could I give? When they asked busy folk who had offered up their hearts, homes and time to dogs who had previously suffered the cruelty that humans too often mete out to the innocent; when they spoke to gifted writers who had found in their dog companions their best and sanest muses; when they met and befriended men and women putting themselves on the line every day to find lost climbers, sniff out deadly bombs, or offer succor to abused children, always with a dog or dogs by their sides showing them the path, and all these people said, "of course, we'll contribute," well, what could this former non-lover of dogs say but: Yes!

I find myself being moved most by an impression of silence. There are many words in this book, shaping rich tales that may well bring you to tears, of joy, of sadness, of recognition. But at the heart of these words, and mentioned again and again throughout the collection, is the great value and healing of a silence that speaks louder than words ever could.

It's the silence of a dedicated Labrador stepping lightly through a literal mine field for the man he loves. The silence of a grievously abused Iggie lifting her face to the sun and then turning, with great and wordless courage, for the first time toward the only person who had ever shown her tenderness. It's the silence of a Kelpie sitting on the bed next to a woman whose life was broken, who he could help in no other way but to be there, right there, where she was. The silence of a dog dying in peace and gratitude in the arms of the man, child, woman, whose heart would continue to remain open because of him.

And that generous, benevolent silence has begun to enter me. I find myself hoping, as one of the fine writers who contributed to this book says, that I too can someday be worthy of "that unconditional, constantly-surprised love when I walk through the door for the one thousandth time." As Lon did, I'll look for the companion who I can serve loyally with my heart and my hands, knowing that he or she will unhesitatingly do the same for me. In this new and surprising quest, I'll wait for the right dog to come into my life. I'll do this knowing what I know now about the often magical way this happens between dogs and their humans. For as another writer here said, simply (and this is something she learned from the dog in her life): we have to be willing to wait.

Alexandra Thurman is a freelance medical editor, poet, and writer living in Seattle, Washington. She is a graduate of the MFA program at Vermont College.

Dog

by Marie Anton

"Look at him," said mother. "He doesn't know he's homely."
Perpetual bridegroom leaping fences.

If he were scorned, do you think he would go morose?
Or even worse, get philosophical and try to plunder from the skies
Meanings that could only give him rise to be impatient with his world,
To question why he lives, and living he must die?

When he first opened sleepy eyes, his nose proclaimed him Prince of Joy.
Life's exclamation! And what if his rump has met a heel or two along the way?
Ecstasy lies one aromatic trunk ahead. And underfoot. And in the air.
And everywhere. All scented things alive or dead are his domain. Conquistador!

Have you no pride, cur? Don't know the wretch you are? Well, I tell you, you are
Hopeless. You think love is blind. I see your grinning shadow running on the wall
As you go trotting by, your little shadow feet, your hairless shadow tail held high –
Never at half-mast –in pursuit of something or other. Back and forth you come and go

With such elan, so confident are you of bliss. I've seen you barking
On the corner with the boys – a motley congress – at old tires and scraps
Of paper in the wind. All doomed, you undepressed canine, the same as we,
Who are so far ahead of you in schemes and metaphysics.

We search, we scour our souls, but cannot find our *now.*
Oh, there you are again. And you've found your *now,* your Heaven
In a reeking bone, exhumed and buried a dozen times or more... .
Well, you go chew on that, my friend, while I gnaw contention's bone.

Gander at Arlington National Cemetery

The Voices at Arlington

by Lon Hodge

"What most separates dogs from humankind isn't mental capacity, however, but innocence. This innocence carries with it a clarity of perception that allows dogs to glory in the wonder of creation in even the most humble scene and quiet moment the combination of their innocence and their intelligence allows them to serve as a bridge between what is transient and what is eternal, between the finite and the infinite." ¨Dean Koontz

Gander, my service dog, and I frequent veteran cemeteries and memorials when we travel. We accept requests in advance from friends and social media; contacts will ask us to visit a relative's gravesite, take a picture of a name on a memorial or leave something in memoriam. Gander quietly sits vigil as I prepare for the rites I have promised to perform. I take this ritual seriously and Gander honors the gravity of promise fulfillment with exceptional calm and professionalism.

Because of the solemnity of our intentions, we go when few people are likely to be there with us at the same time. But, more than once we have exchanged whispered greetings along the way with others and have occasionally been invited into emotional drawing rooms: that place between the living and the dead where Gold Star families mourn. Twice, while at Arlington National Cemetery, Gander has called people deep in grief out of their sadness and comforted them as they spoke about love and loss.

I think we often see and hear what we want to see and hear; we interpret simple events as important lessons. And at other times life really does conjure up for us exactly what we need, at that moment in time, to navigate toward safety and comfort; a last chance at rescue before resigning ourselves to being adrift forever.

Gander had stopped unexpectedly several times. He would look to me for approval and then gaze out toward the long rows of white markers. Then he would cock his head the way a dog does when someone is talking to him.

A women and her daughter who had been ahead of us for most of our journey toward the Tomb of the Unknown Soldier stopped just a few yards short of our destination. "Do you suppose he can hear them? The soldiers?" I was relieved. It wasn't just me who thought he was in touch with something invisible and inaudible to humans. It was a beautiful sunny day. There was a slight breeze, but it was barely strong enough to rustle leaves. He looked engaged, not perplexed or curious in the same caring way he connects with me when I need a dispassionate listener in times of inner turmoil.

She told me that she visits Arlington once a week. Her brother was interred not far away. He'd served in Vietnam as a hospital corpsman. His Purple Heart was earned with a minor injury when their mobile surgery facility was mortared one dark midnight in 1969. He'd been given the Silver Star for his selfless actions that same night while attending to patients without regard for his own welfare. She shared that he had left both medals at the base of Vietnam Memorial years ago as a tribute to the dozens of men he had watched succumb to injuries beyond medicine's ability to repair.

The day his tour ended he was taken by helicopter from a fire base where he had been performing triage, deciding who would stand the best chance of quick treatment, for wounded members of a platoon that experienced heavy casualties when ambushed by the Viet Cong. He was transported to a waiting 727 that flew him to San Francisco where, still in jungle fatigues, he disembarked through a gauntlet of angry protesters. At twenty years old he was a stranger in his own country after only nine months in Vietnam.

He'd been afraid when he went, she said. The fear was replaced by the grief and guilt he felt on his return. She told me that he remembered every name, and held pictures in his mind of every wound he had dressed. His world became television, books, and a dozen ways to pass the sleepless hours.

For many years, a job in the post office on the graveyard shift kept him financially solvent. He never applied for Veterans benefits. Working at night, there were few people who demanded his attention. But, the anxiety and depression worsened. And isolation couldn't create enough new memories to replace the old ones.

By the time he reached out for help, the VA, with the casualties of two new wars to attend to, had few programs and little time to coax cooperation from an aging Viet Vet. The new counselor hires were kind enough, but they couldn't empathize with a man, decades their senior, who could barely give voice to the increasing sadness and despair inside of him.

He left a note the day he hung himself. He said the only reliable friend left in his life was suicide. He asked not to be buried in a military cemetery because that was reserved for soldiers who fought and for those he'd watched over as they died. But, because money was tight she had arranged for him to be interred at Arlington.

"I feel ashamed. I want him to be at peace," she said quietly. "Do you think he can ever forgive me?"

You want to say "yes" at moments like that. You want to have a spiritual connection; you want to believe that this kind of deadly regret can be vanquished. That another good person should die physically, emotionally or spiritually because they had done the best they could, should never happen.

I want to lie just to give her some peace. But, remorse and grief are clever, intuitive adversaries: They know when you have nothing more to offer than a "sorry" in the way of an anecdote, aphorism or falsehood meant to send them on their way. I had courted suicide for a long time. There, but for the grace of Gander and God, was I. But, I couldn't do it. I didn't know what to do or say.

Just then, Gander rose, turned again toward the graves, before slowly moving toward me with his head bowed. He reared back on his hind legs and placed his front paws squarely in the center of my chest and looked me straight in the eyes the way he does when I am overwhelmed and at a loss for words or actions. A long kiss on the cheek later and he pushed himself off, wheeling to turn toward the woman, who by now was in tears. He turned his body sideways and leaned his weight against her.

It hardly matters whether or not it was coincidence that Gander chose that moment to be affectionate. It has happened so many times now I am no longer surprised when it happens. There was no explanation needed, no words left to be exchanged between us. She did lean down to look into Gander's endlessly soulful eyes to say "thank you". We both received an answer we could believe.

Dog Park in the Morning

by Robert W. Hill

Reeking of slobber and sweat, I am
on my way to talk poems with friends.

Late, of course, I thought, This is a poem
in the making. All that rush and bother

reaching with dirty hands toward peace
and quiet in clean words on bright paper.

But it's the wrong day, so I am twenty-five
hours early and tinkering with "slobber and sweat"

at a library computer. I have had good days
in those conditions, making do with error,

like walking into wet concrete while reading
Calvino, or envisioning the sultry death of

quicksand in a Tarzan movie. Not that those
are errors, but surrounded by time without

direction, blinking away not an instant but
half a day, until wiggling my toes while sitting

cannot stave off the left hip-pain or the butt-itch
and thirst, and hunger. Sometimes, standing in dust

and heat, with rising shit-smell, the dog park
feels like time itself, flowing hills, all downward,

until the long climb back up a raggedy lawn
with, oh, for sure, dogs of every sort, colliding

by accident in running-joy, snarling and sniffing
to everyone's satisfaction, privacy gone and priority

established like a psalm, those that gut the pretense,
situate the guilt in glare, and levitate a final prayer.

"He is your friend, your partner, your defender, your dog. You are his life, his love, his leader. He will be yours, faithful and true, to the last beat of his heart. You owe it to him to be worthy of such devotion."
-- Author Unknown

Corky the Corgi

by Ian Hubbard

A little more than three years ago, my family and I adopted a Pembroke Welsh Corgi we named Corky. She was an adult dog at the time we got her, but we think she was in a puppy mill when she was younger. When she came to live with us, we learned quickly that this little dog had a huge personality. We also learned that she was born to run. Corky died last October from an unexpected injury, and I still feel angry and sad that she is gone. But in the short time she lived with us, she created a lifetime of memories.

I still can't think of Corky without thinking of food. One time, she hopped up on the table and snatched a sandwich that was supposed to be mine. I can't blame her, though, because it was from Five Guys! No one would call Corky a picky eater, something we learned after we took her for a walk and she gobbled up a truly disgusting piece of pizza someone had dropped on the sidewalk. She was also adventurous when it came to beverages. One day she jumped onto a chair and put her front paws on the table, and then slurped some of Mom's coffee. When we came in the dining room, Corky looked at us, happily: "Morning, Family"!

In fact, Corky was pretty much a fur ball of pure happiness. She created her own game called "Catch-a-Bunny," and she succeeded at doing that at least three times! She could run like a speeding cheetah, and she had reflexes, hearing, eyesight, and a nose like no other. She played football with my dad and me, but her rules were a little different than ours. She couldn't catch the ball, but she seemed to think that if she wanted it, it should be hers. I don't know why, but we never argued with her interpretation!

Corky had some difficult personality traits, but her heart was very sweet. She loved us, and it always made me smile when we'd return home and see that she was looking out the front window, watching for our return. When the family would pile on the bed to watch a movie, I loved it when she would lick my feet. She was also a snuggler, especially when it rained and she was scared, or she needed comfort. Corky's face looked a little like a fox's, and there was always a smile on it, even to the very end.

A dog's life can be harder than ours, and I'm sure that Corky's started out very hard. From start to finish, our courageous dog tried her best to be loved. She may not have gotten love in her first few years, but when she came to live with our family, we definitely gave her every kind of love we could think of was food, shelter, companionship, petting and snuggles, and because it was Corky, more food! She gave us so much love back, it was like she'd saved it up from all those hard years when there was no love around.

She changed us and made us more understanding and patient when we had to deal with some of her bad habits, like nipping and herding. In our hearts, we will always hold a special place for our Corky. We'll remember her forever.

"Dogs are our link to paradise. They don't know evil or jealousy or discontent. To sit with a dog on a hillside on a glorious afternoon is to be back in Eden, where doing nothing was not boring--it was peace."
-- Milan Kundera

The Duchess and Sarge

by Jim Poland

I lifted Dad up in my arms from his comfy, swivel rocker and carried him down the hall to place him gently into the hospital bed that had just arrived within the hour. At his

feet Duchess had, as always, been lying curled up. She loyally walked alongside me, waited in the doorway until I had Dad situated in his new bed with his oxygen hose re-looped over his ears and under his nose and then curled back up underneath his bed to keep him company.

My father retired at the rank of Master Sargeant from the US Air Force with twenty-three years combined service. He had joined the Army shortly after high school graduation in June of 1942, just seven months after the Japanese attack at Pearl Harbor. Like most members of his generation, he rarely talked about his years in the Pacific Theatre "landing on almost every island" and serving as a small arms armorer with his partner, Shorty, the farm boy from Iowa, as they drove their deuce and a half to support forward Marine units. He told me he never considered himself a combat veteran, although when asked he described being shelled, ambushed, and sniped at during his "trips to support the boys". Sarge went to Korea after the war to prep equipment for shipping back to Stateside. Once he returned home to the countryside of Massachusetts, he realized he yearned for the Service and seeing the world and enlisted in the newly minted Air Force.

As his cancer progressed and we spent time waiting for the docs, the results, and during occasional hours-long stays in the ER, he shared more about his youth than about his war days. That still impresses me, since he served two tours in country during the Korean War and was in a Minuteman silo awaiting "orders from the President to launch our missile at Cuba" in October, 1962. When Dad retired, the Vietnam War was still raging and after struggling to work in the "private sector", he spent fifteen more years serving our nation as an ATF inspector utilizing his military experience.

Duchess only left Dad's side that first night to visit the lawn and take a drink of water. As I sat next to Dad in his non-communicative, semi-conscious state, Duchess laid her head on my feet and would occasionally glance from me to him as if to ask me when he was getting up.

That's when I saw the picture on his dresser. The picture was of a boy no older than ten and a curly-haired Golden Retriever playing in front of some apple trees. The trees were on his grandparents' property where he lived with his parents during the Great Depression.

When I had asked him about the picture and remarked how much Duchess looked like the dog in the picture, Dad had said that some of his happiest memories during the years of his family's struggles during the Depression were with that dog. He had had a goat and chickens, but it was his loyal dog that warmed his memories of his youth and comforted him. That picture held a prominent position on his dresser the last years of his life, as Duchess provided him with the unconditional love and loyalty that he needed to help through his struggles with his failing heart, the progression of his cancer, and the weakness brought on by the damage of polio to his muscles in his twenties.

Duchess dutifully accompanied her Sarge on road trips to the store, and to the park to walk with me and my pup. Duchess kept Dad mobile, exercised and more youthful in the seven years they shared together. It was obvious, as it was this night as I sat gazing at my father and listening to his labored breathing, that Duchess gave her Sarge joy and Sarge gave Duchess all that a dog could ask for in a good home.

Dad enjoyed pampering Duchess with fresh cooked vegetables and other healthy treats. He discovered that she enjoyed fresh vegetables so much that she would happily eat tomatoes and green and red bell peppers right off the plants in his garden in the backyard. And Dad had told me that he got frustrated with Duchess when she chased the birds and rabbits from his yard, but he understood that she was a retriever and field dog from birth. My wife and I never told him in the Spring of his last year that we discovered that Duchess would also shake a small tree to cause baby birds to fall out of the nest and to our horror snatch them up for a seeming snack.

For four days and nights, Duchess slept under Dad's bed, barely leaving his side but for a quick trip in the yard and a drink of water and food. When Dad's labored breathing came to an end and he had passed, she would no longer enter his bedroom, but instead lay down at the room's doorway as if to guard his body.

My wife had realized some weeks earlier that Dad was worried about Duchess's fate and she had assured him that she would always have a loving home with us. When it came time for Duchess to come home with us, I had to carry her to the car because she refused to leave her home on the hill with her Sarge.

Duchess lived a great life for three more years with us and our chocolate lab, Cookie, who she knew very well. She seemed happy enough, but never content. She always seemed to be waiting for her Sarge to come pick her up and take her home with him. Which eventually, he did.

Green Berets: Live and Die by the Wag of a Tail

by Kevin Hanrahan

Cold, thick air swirled in front of US Army Specialist John Nolan's face, disappearing into the blue Afghanistan sky as his heart pounded. Surely the eight Green Berets he was patrolling with him could hear his heart pounding? He swore it must sound like the bass drum of a marching band.

The Wilkes-Barre, Pennsylvania native watched as his partner, Specialized Search Dog (SSD) Honza "Bear", lumber through the two-foot deep snow, surging in front of the men and into the wadi fearlessly searching for explosives. Explosives that could detonate anytime killing them both instantly.

Did "The Bear" ever get scared, John wondered?

His 100-pound yellow-furred partner's tail was wagging, nose low, and John could hear the crunching snow as Honza searched the ground. Honza didn't look scared. Damn dog looked like he was having fun.

If he wasn't scared, then John shouldn't be either. They had already been through so much together. It had been an epic ride ever since meeting one another at dog school. "Why me?" thought John as he looked around at the other eleven students in his specialized search dog school at Lackland Air Force Base, Texas one year earlier. The other guys were looking at each another, smiling, laughing and joking. He wished he could have shared their enthusiasm.

"We've tried him before with four other SSD students and he never works out," his instructors had informed him. This is not what the three-year-and-one-combat-deployment Army veteran had expected when he volunteered for K9 School. Why couldn't he have one of the other guys' "good" dogs instead of this washout, wondered John as he shuffled his feet down the kennel walkway.

"That's him right there, Nolan. That big goofy Labrador Retriever is yours."

John sighed heavily and turned to face his new partner, the partner that he would be relying on to find improvised explosives before they found him. He turned with his hands on his hips and stared at the unimpressive yellow dog who barely acknowledged his presence. John looked up at his name plate above his kennel. It read "Honza, 4YO, male."

Honza let out a yawn, looked up at him and seemed to be saying, "I've been through this before with other handlers. I sabotaged them and I'll do the same to you. Let's get this over with so I can lounge around."

John's shoulders tensed as he reached for the kennel door and opened it. Honza got to his feet. John took a step forward into the cage, and was quickly pushed backwards before landing on his rear end with Honza on top of him. Honza'a massive front paws were on his chest and his wet slimy pink tongue was lathering John's face with saliva.

John wrapped his arms around the dog, squeezing him and pulling him into a tight hug. He could feel the dog's heart pounding and then Honza groaned with delight as he tried to lick John's face some more. He groaned like a bear. John could feel their connection.

Why had Honza never worked out with any other handler, John wondered?

Two days later John had found out exactly what was wrong when they ran their first search drill. Honza took three times the amount of time to complete the exercise as the other dogs did. He was slow, lethargic, appeared to be out for a Sunday stroll rather than looking for explosives. Honza had no sense of urgency.

John watched him curiously and thought that he looked like an unwieldy bear, poking around for snacks at a campsite. Paw this and paw that. He would sniff here and there, stroll to the left or right and sniff again, look at a passing butterfly and then take a few more steps with his nose down. His long yellow tail wagged from side to side as if it were a windshield wiper on a rainy day. He was Honza the Bear!

"Don't worry, Nolan. He'll be your backup dog. We are giving you another dog tomorrow," his instructor informed him.

John looked up at the staff sergeant instructor and wanted to ask, "What if I don't want another dog? What if I want Honza Bear to be my dog?" But he kept his mouth shut.

His instructors were true to their word and paired him with a second dog, Lucy, a combat veteran who had completed two tours of duty with the Marines. Honza may have been his "backup dog" but John's heart was already committed. John had made the cardinal mistake at dog school. He had fallen in love instantly with this big goofy knuckleheaded Labrador.

John spent his free time working with Honza on basics and then they gradually moved to the obedience (obstacle) course. Obedience is the most important fundamental of a working dog and his handler. It helps build that critical bond between the two. John also began conducting all kennel care for Honza. If Honza wanted food, water, out of his kennel...then he needed John.

One day during training, John's senior instructor pulled him aside after watching him and Honza work a training problem and asked, "Nolan, what have you done to Honza? I've never seen him work this well for anyone else. Heck, I've never seen him work this well, period."

John was elated and replied, "He just gets me Sergeant. And I get him. He may be slow, but he's thorough. I'm okay with him being thorough when we're searching for things that could blow us up." As his instructor walked away John knelt down to pet Honza who had flipped over on his back. As John stroked his belly Honza began making grumbling noises that sounded, yep, like a bear.

Honza Bear was starting to come around, but by the end of the course there was still no doubt that Lucy was a better search dog. John's instructors urged him to choose her instead of Honza. But John's heart belonged to The Bear. When John departed dog school for Virginia it was that big yellow head sticking out of his car, ears flapping, tongue hanging in the breeze. John was going to take his chances with The Bear.

Now, that chance was in Afghanistan, where eight other American was relying on the pair to keep them alive.

"He's earned your trust. Have faith in The Bear, Nolan," John told himself. "Get your ass down into that wadi with your partner. "

After only two steps an anxious pulse surged though John's body as Honza jerked back. That was his change of behavior. John knew The Bear had caught a whiff of something dangerous.

As Honza worked the odor, John followed him cautiously, stepping exactly where Honza had, watching his dog's every move. His chances of not getting blown up were better if he followed Honza's paw prints with his boot prints. But nothing was guaranteed. Hell, they had barely made it out of Virginia. They were barely a certified dog team. They had failed their first attempt in miserable fashion because Honza had reverted back to the form.

And then, two weeks before they were scheduled to deploy the team's second attempt at certification, they had spent an epic four days in Virginia that John would never forget. "Listen, Bear. We can't afford to fail. This is serious. We need to pass certification so we can go to Afghanistan and protect our troops," John had said as he pinched Honza's lips together and pulled the dog's face close to his. Almost immediately, he wished his tone had been softer. Honza began to growl. "Do you understand me, Bear?"

Honza's growl got louder, a deep series of low, piercing belly growls, definitely directed at John. Honza pulled his head back, freeing his lips from John's grasp. When John was called out for the in-brief, Honza began pawing at the door . He barked loudly as John left for the in-brief, those brown eyes burning a hole in John's back.

Three days later Honza was no longer lumbering. He was rumbling along at a pace John had never seen him work before. John had poked The Bear.

They easily passed the first trials and were breezing through certification. Until the last trial, when Honza moved so fast during the building search that he ran right past the explosive training aides. He missed everything. They had failed again. Was this the end of John's partnership with Honza Bear? Would they be removed from the dog program? John's head was numb, his stomach in revolt. He slumped onto the ground and fought back tears. Honza sniffed his face and rubbed his warm nose on John's. John pulled him tightly against his chest. He couldn't lose The Bear.

He held his dog in his arms for well over an hour. He watched the other dog teams come back from the problem with smiles of their faces, both dogs and men. He wanted to feel the way they did.

"Nolan, go see Master Sergeant Hathaway to receive your score," said another handler.

John shuffled his feet as he moved slowly towards Hathaway, the certification authority. He already knew they had failed.

"All right, Nolan. You guys have been solid all week. I'm giving you one more chance to successfully navigate this trial," Hathaway said.

John heart leaped as he nodded his head. "Roger, Master Sergeant."

He knelt down next to The Bear as he unleashed him and said, "This is it, buddy. I need you, pal. I can't lose you."

Honza looked back at him with his lips caught in his bottom teeth. He leaned back on his hind legs, stretched out his front and placed his head between his front paws. His tail wouldn't stop wagging.

John could have sworn The Bear was smiling at him. "Seek!"

Honza bolted out of his stance and dashed down the hallway of the barracks. He ran all the way to the end of the hall, sniffed the bottom of a door seam and dropped his butt to the floor.

John hesitated for a minute. "Seriously, Honza, you on scent that quickly?" he thought. He knew this was it. They were passing or failing right there.

"He's on it, Master Sergeant. Good boy, Honza. Good boy. Who's my buddy, huh, Honza?"

As he "paid" Honza, he prayed that they weren't wrong. With trepidation, John looked over at Hathaway, whose stoic face relaxed into a big grin.

"Good job, Nolan. Good luck in Afghanistan." He shook John's hand, patted Honza on the head and walked away, leaving John stunned. They had passed!

But that had been training with explosive aids on a stateside Army base. Now they were looking for real explosives with a real enemy trying to kill them in an alien land. Running past an explosive, missing one, one wrong step, and they wouldn't just fail a test. Unless you called staying alive a test.

Honza already had three explosive finds in Afghanistan. Three times already, John and the others had returned safely to their combat outpost because of Honza.

Now the dog was back on the scent. There was definitely something here, and John could easily set it off by stepping on it.

"We have something. Back up"! John hollered to the Green Beret team.

Honza Bear's nose went high left, then low left, then high right, then low left, then right trying to pinpoint where the IED was. He let out a low growl and John could sense his frustration.

"Relax Nolan. Trust The Bear," John kept repeating in his head.

The scent of explosives seemed to be everywhere and John knew Honza was having trouble determining the exact location of the source. The six inches of snow wasn't helping. John froze in place. He was done testing the ground with his own weight. If the explosives were rigged to be set off by a pressure plate then they would both be blown to pieces.

Honza moved swiftly back towards John. He sniffed around his feet and looked up. John could see what looked like anguish in his partner's eyes. The thought that maybe this was his day to die entered his mind.

Then Honza took two steps forward and sat down. That was his final response. Honza was telling him he had found the explosive source.

John was only about a foot from where Honza was showing that the explosive was buried. He stared back at Honza, trying to decide if he was actually "on odor" or had sat down out of frustration.

But Honza's tail was flopping back and forth faster than a windshield wiper in a downpour.

"Trust in The Bear," he told himself again.

John knew this wasn't a false alarm. Honza was "on odor." It was time to praise Honza and get them both the hell out of there.

But Honza's tail kept wagging, wagging, and as it wagged, it brushed the snow away from a dark object now only partially covered by the snow. As John prepared to step forward toward his partner, he could now clearly see something shining like a beacon in the white snow right where he was about to step. It was a goddamn doorbell ringer attached to a 9-volt battery. John could see wires connected to it. He knew where those wires went.

Right to the explosives that would have sent him home in a pine box.

The doorbell was the Improvised Explosive Device's initiator. He would have walked right onto the device if it hadn't been for Honza Bear's determined and effective tail. Honza Bear had saved them all again.

John knew they might not be so lucky the next time. But nothing would deter Specialist John Nolan and Honza Bear from the task they were committed to: One day at a time, one explosive device at a time, they would keep their Green Beret brothers alive.

John Nolan and Honza in Afghanistan

The Color of Courage: Red

by Lynn Bukowski

This is what it feels like to watch someone I love fall out of the sky: I tilt my head back, shield my eyes from sunglow, and watch tiny specks drop from a plane so high, I cannot actually see it in the cerulean blue sky. I only hear a distant drone. Big Red, our 120 pound Golden Retriever, begins to pace around my legs in a tight circle. The behavior is so unusual for this markedly obedient dog that I sense something is off, but I keep my eyes skyward, fascinated now by a long, colorful cloth spiraling up from one of the floating dots. The silk flaps around like a rag doll; whips at the sky, but does not catch the wind. Red stops pacing and emits a long, fretful sound somewhere between a moan and a bark. The Platoon Chief beside me angles his binoculars just so and shouts "Buk!" my husband's nickname.

My throat closes, my breath stops and the chatter around me turns heavy and distorted. I lock my knees because standing seems impossible and blessedly, Red is solid against my left side. I lean into him. The spiraling cloth crumbles away and it is agonizing moments before a small chute mushrooms out, catches the wind and snaps dangling legs to attention. Still, Steve is dropping far too fast. I do not even have time to make an entire "deal" with God before Red bolts from my side and runs flat out toward the drop zone. This is against all rules and some small part of my brain thinks of calling him back, but I don't. Instead, I watch as, if in slow motion, Red skids sideways into two black boots a microsecond before they hit ground. Legs fold like a dance movement and two bodies (large dog and man) drop into a long controlled roll, tumbling over and over before they both pop upright, tangled in line and parachute. I glimpse Steve hunched over, hands on his knees with Red beside him, panting. The men around me cheer, curse, and run. I drop to my knees, then to all fours as the air leaves my lungs and the world turns black.

This is where they find me. I half-wake to a mixture of dust and dog breath. Red laps his long wet tongue up the middle of my face. From a distance I hear, "Happy Anniversary, honey." Both Steve and Red are grinning (I'm sure) as though this impromptu anniversary gift, indeed, the world tilting on its edge, is hysterical.

That was my third anniversary gift and to this day – decades later - I'm sure Big Red saved my husband's life that day. Of course, the law of physics might not support my certainty, but believe me, it was just the beginning of this courageous dog's gift.

We adopted Big Red shortly after our first son was born. Every kid needs a dog and we fell in love with his sparkling brown eyes and deep red coat of fur. We were told Red was bred to win top prizes in dog shows. But his head was too big according to some ridiculous rule, and at just over a year old, he was dumped with a Retriever Rescue Group. None of us – the rescue group – or our naïve young family – realized the extent of Red's training until years later, but looking back, it was glaringly obvious.

From the first night in our home, Red *adopted* our baby son. He politely watched me place his new dog bed in a corner of the kitchen and after a quick drink, curled up and lay down. He watched as we ate dinner, during baby bath-time and story reading, but as we tucked our little one into his crib, Red left the room and returned dragging his dog bed by his mouth. He carefully placed it at the end of the crib and Red's bed (or new versions of it) remained in that spot through 16 babies (two homemade, 1 adopted and 13 foster babies) and seven different homes across the country. On his own, Red taught each of our children how to walk him before they were big enough to see over his back. No kidding, he would retrieve his leash from a basket and heel to their little steps around the back yard.

With an uncanny sense, Red always knew to be gentle with children and outright frightening to unwelcome strangers. Often, when Steve was deployed, I would watch Red's reaction *before* opening the front door to someone unknown. He was right one hundred percent of the time.

On one occasion, I was distracted and opened the door to our foster daughter's new boyfriend. Before I had a chance to say hello, Red sped past me, jumped at the boy and had his jaw locked around the young man's right arm, then twisted until the kid fell to his knees, screaming. I froze in horror for a brief moment – until I saw the weapon – and then, with far more bravado then I felt, lifted the gun out of his useless hand and called the police. Red held the boy down the entire time, releasing only when the police arrived.

But the most memorable save happened during Red's last year of life. Our youngest son was only an infant and barely two month's old – attached 24 hours a day to a heart and apnea monitor, which alerted with loud beeps when his heart or breathing stopped. Most of the time, the alerts would require only minimal stimulation for Aaron to respond, and the family (including Red) was well used to the sound. In 1991, Red suffered from arthritis and was partially blind, so he stayed on his bed a good portion of each day. That particular day, during naptime, I decided to vacuum and was nearly done with the upstairs when Red ran from the bedroom and grabbed my hand with his jaw.

He growled and whined and pulled, and the instant I turned off the vacuum I heard the alarm of Aaron's monitor. Aaron was nearly blue and I had to administer CPR and simultaneously phone for help. Red stayed by my side the entire time. Aaron is now a 22 year old, six foot four inch, handsome young man. Red passed away 11 months later on his bed at the end of Aaron's crib, exactly one week after Aaron was well enough to go without his heart and apnea monitors and sleep through the night.

I think he planned it that way.

Wanker

by Stephanie Weaver

This British term has evolved to mean someone who is a naughty smartass, full of piss and vinegar. It became one of my dog Buddy Girl's nicknames, as she had a wanky side that was simultaneously frustrating and endearing.

Overall, she was well behaved, but there were times when she was just plain contrary. The thing about having a bright dog is that, not only do they *know* when they're yanking your chain, they know that YOU know that they're yanking your chain. You can see it in their eyes, and it drives you nuts.

Golden Retrievers are bred to follow you out hunting, stay by your side, not bolt when you shoot a bird, run to the dead bird on command, pick it up gently (as opposed to ripping it to shreds), bring it back, and drop it at your feet. That's a lot of smarts and breeding. If you don't give them a job, they tend to get bored, destructive, or take over the house. They need tons of exercise and lots of training. If you do all that, they are simply awesome.

Most of the time, Buddy Girl was pretty awesome. Except when she was being a wanker.

Her favorite toys were stolen ones. A houseful of kids lives next door, so there is always something juicy in that yard: tiny stuffed animals, balls, rawhides. She would trot over there, steal something, and then trot back home. Buddy always had to show you that she'd stolen something; that was part of the fun. She would mock-growl at you, turning her head from side to side until you noticed and commented on whatever she had in her mouth. If you advanced towards her, she'd trot to her bed to worry whatever she'd picked up. It was a constant game. She'd bring stuff into the house. I'd let her play with it, and then eventually toss it back next door, like a fisherman tossing back a little fish.

When she was little, we hung a bell on each side of the back door and taught her to ring it to go out and come back in. That way she could tell us when she needed to go out without a bark. Except... she figured out it was way more fun to ring to go out, then ring to come in, then ring to go out. Down came the bells. Wanker.

One way we kept her bright little brain occupied was to create enrichment toys. Her favorite was a water bottle with a hole cut in it, just big enough for pieces of kibble to come out. She would roll it around, working the puzzle to earn her snack. Then she got a little older and figured out how to get the cap off in about five seconds and she'd carry it back for a refill. Wanker.

In a dog pack, the leader gets the highest position. So you're not supposed to have dogs sleep up on a bed or couch at your level. We followed that rule, except we really loved cuddling with her. So we would let her get up on our lap, but only her two front paws. Every once in a while, she'd arrange herself so that she could creep that third leg up, just to see if we'd notice it dangling in the breeze. One day she maneuvered herself right up into my chair with me. She was so surprised by this she didn't quite know what to do, but she tried to make herself comfortable. I was laughing so hard I could hardly breathe. Might have been the 75-pound dog circling on my lap, heavy paws poking my organs as she stepped!

Her favorite game was Keep Away. This was a product of first-time dog owners (us) who failed to give proper training early on. She played Keep Away with us, and with other dogs. That was fine, so long as a) it was our ball and not theirs, b) it was a ball and not a baby's toy, c) she didn't have both our ball AND their ball in her mouth. Wanker.

The biggest problem was that retrieving was optional in her book. Most retrievers love to retrieve, so they will come to you and drop it every time so that you will THROW IT AGAIN. Bud wasn't like that. She liked running after it, up to a point. Then she might decide to go visit someone, pick up a pine cone to chew, or simply lie down in the shade. You'd fling the ball for her and she'd look at you and you could almost hear her say, "Wow. That's kinda far. I don't think so. Why don't you go get it? That pine cone looks delicious," as she walked over to the pine tree and flopped down in the needles, leaving you to walk across the entire park to retrieve her ball. Wanker.

But by far the most wankery thing she did was refuse to drop the ball. All the dogs in our area play with these high-pitched squeaky balls that make them go crazy, nicknamed "crack balls." Dogs that don't *like* balls love them. Dogs that *don't play with toys* love them. And retrievers LOVE them. I've seen black Labs get so excited they've swallowed them whole. Not only are they piercingly squeaky, they fly far if properly flung by a Chuck-it, and they make a satisfyingly squishy sound when covered with slobber. Bud would run like the wind for one of her squeakers, but she would never give it up.

We tried everything, including turkey bacon. She wasn't interested in food or treats when she was young, so they only worked up to a point for training. She would drop it five times in a row for the turkey bacon. And then, on return number six, you'd see that look in her eye and you'd know that she was weighing the choice between keeping the ball in her mouth and another sliver of turkey bacon. The ball would win. Wanker.

One trainer told us that dogs don't like peppermint, and when positive reinforcements no longer work you can use breath spray, a tiny squirt in the mouth. That was the only thing that worked. It worked so well that all I had to do was pull it out of my pocket and she would drop the ball. So long as I remembered my breath spray, all was well. I'd chuck the ball, she'd retrieve it most of the way, I'd convince her to finish coming to me, I'd wave the breath spray at her, she'd drop it, I'd fling it again.

All was well until one day a dog trainer started coming to our park. His dog was impressively well trained in Germany, and he gave me a hard time about the breath spray. I explained that we'd tried everything and she would not give up the squeaker. He told me that he could train her to drop it. I said, "Please! Go for it!" I was curious to see if he could.

The first throw, with his Dog-Whisperish-Pack-Leader demeanor, Buddy dropped it right away. Damn! The second time, instant drop. Wow, maybe he *can* train her! The third time, a hesitation, then a drop. Excellent. The fourth time, I saw the look in her eyes and thought, "Uh oh."

He tried to get it out of her mouth. She clamped down on his hand. He wedged his fingers in there. She clamped harder. He pried her jaws apart and, after what stretched into a long wrestling match, finally extracted the ball, breathing heavily. Hmm.

Now he needed to cement his dominance. To show her who was boss, he threw it again and commanded her to fetch it. She trotted off, picked it up, and started heading for home without so much as a look back. And that was that. It was breath spray or nothing.

Wanker.

Remembering Molly: My Teacher

by Lynn Rasmussen

"We can fix her!" The veterinarian said, confidently.

His voice echoed around the hard surfaces of the vet's examination room. It sounded loud and stiff to me, and it did nothing to steady my already jangled nerves. Excellent, I thought, *they* can fix her and then *we* can get back to our lives and *I* don't have to face the aging of my beloved German Shepherd Dog, Molly.

Years earlier, when Molly was much younger, and after I'd decided that Molly was the ideal candidate for a working Therapy Dog, she and I worked towards and earned our Delta Society Pet Partners Therapy Dog license. I still remember the handwritten note on the exam paperwork, from one of the reviewers, "Nice Team!" Of all the tests and trials we went through to obtain our license, I think that observation was the one of which I was the most proud. Once we had our license with our photo on it, and after we received our 'Working Dog Vest' …well, I'll admit it – we thought we were the bee's knees! Molly's 'Working Dog Vest' was like a superhero's cape from out of a Marvel Comic-book, and the license seemed like the key to Fort Knox - announcing to the world, [to the tune of the Mighty Mouse cartoon …], "Here-we-are-to-save-the-day!" Once we were an official team, outfitted and ready to do battle against sadness, loneliness, and emotionally-worn-out-people-everywhere; Molly and I were inseparable. She and I now spent almost as much time together as a Military Working Dog team, or a Service Dog team.

As with a child, any mother will agree that their child often 'orbits' around them; and Molly always orbited around me. When I reached my hand out, I knew it would come to rest on the head of my furry planetary body. Inseparable. That is, until October, 2009, when I noticed that Molly was struggling to rise from her usual resting spot against the antique dry-sink.

A week later, I found myself slouched on the floor of the veterinarian's exam room, sitting against a cold door-stop mounted on the wall and feeling its pain in my hip. I only vaguely noticed the pain it was causing, though, since my heart was racing, making my breath come in shallow, quiet gasps…the vet had bad news. Molly was sitting in the opposite corner, looking hard at me.

"So, what's wrong with her?" I asked the vet in a breathless voice. It seemed hard to get the words out.

"Well, her hip bone is degenerating and it'll have to be fixed surgically. We have a procedure for that; it's got a very good success rate. Until we can get her into the surgery, we can give her steroids to keep her going," he said, matter-of-factly.

Very efficient. Very clean. Very painless. We trust our vet, we love him … he's been part of our 'team' for over 20 years. However, vets don't live on Mount Olympus - they do the best they can to save lives and to make lives worth living. The clinical notes from the entire team of medical professionals working on Molly were indicative of a successful procedure. The problem had been identified; a plan of action laid out and a solution was on the horizon. Go Team! Why then, did I have the sense I was walking on thin ice? You know the feeling… every muscle tense…ready, preparing at every step to be plunged into the dark world of a frozen pond. It was like being in a battle, but I wasn't in a battle. Was I? I suddenly realized that Molly was 13 years old.

From somewhere inside me, a thin voice chirped up, "We can do it! We can fix her! Come on, all the medical people have testified that this is a successful procedure! We can go to physical therapy and go back to work as a Therapy Dog Team! She's only 13 years old! Do it, do it, do it!" The voice sounded like a politician, thin, high-pitched and full of an adrenaline that made it quiver. But it had done its job; we would proceed with the surgery.

While Molly was in surgery, I went about my day, but I felt as if I was walking in a dream – seeing, but not seeing. All I could really see were visions of my early days with Molly. Long forgotten, they now focused in front of me like a scene through a clearing fog.

We adopted Molly in the spring of 1998, when she was 10 months old. She had been in 4 homes in those 10 months. She had lived all over the state of North Carolina and had been summarily dumped at a shelter. She was rescued by the German Shepherd Rescue & Adoptions (GSRA). I saw her at a GSRA Adoption Event; she was at the end of a long line of beautiful German Shepherd Dogs, with her head hanging low, her right ear flopping to the side, making her head look like a broken, sad, goofy numeral "4".

"I'll take HER!" I said excitedly, pointing to Molly.

I didn't know it then, but I had just found my best friend. For twelve-and-a-half years, she was the one with whom I spent more time than even my own husband. Molly looked to me for everything. She was emotionally wrecked when she came to me. She was afraid of everything, and had no confidence or spiritual strength. She spent the first week at our home sitting in the corner of the mudroom. I knew it was my job to care for her, to solve her problems and to meet her every need, from the quality of her food to the comfort of her sleep. She looked to me to give her the confidence to approach the dangerous bush next to the driveway; to face down the sparrow inside it.

Molly looked to me to tell her that everything was going to be OK, and she and I formed the strongest of bonds –we trusted each other absolutely. In the years when we were working as a Therapy Dog team, she looked to me to show her how to mount the escalators at the Charlotte Hilton, how to stay out of the way of a wheelchair, and how to be still and quiet under a table during a meeting. But she didn't need to look to me whenever we were working with patients in hospital; she knew who needed her attention. She would pad silently up to the most withdrawn patient in the room and stand there in front of them…staring, as if to say, "It's OK. I'm here now." She would stand firm in front of the patient until the patient reached out for her. That was all her, all Molly; I could never have taught her to do that. When we received our diagnosis that horrible day, I knew I had to fix Molly so she could carry on her work.

But in spite of a gifted medical team, it wouldn't turn out that way

The night before Molly's surgery, snow began to fall unexpectedly. I lay down with her in the family room and we gazed at the falling snow together. The snow was mixed with heavy ice pellets and it was making a muffled pinging noise as it hit the windows. I had my fingers buried in her mane around her neck and shoulders; it was warm and peaceful. I wanted that night to last forever.

Death came for Molly at 6:30 PM on March 9, 2010.

Molly passed in the safety of my arms and in the peace of her back deck in her own backyard, listening to my voice telling her that she would be safe and I would follow her later. "You go ahead, Mol," I said quietly into her ear, like a lullaby. "I'll see you later…it's OK to go now, I promise I'll be there soon," …and I rocked her gently to sleep.

As Molly's chest fell for the last time, I felt nothing but shock and loneliness. Suddenly, there was nothing.

That feeling of nothingness lasted almost three years. There were dark days when I simply wanted to disappear, when the weight of the grief and loneliness was simply crushing. It seemed as if I couldn't get away from the grief. It was like walking through cigarette smoke in the park…you can't see the smoke, but somehow it becomes attached to you….you become wrapped up in it. And it stinks. There was no place to go to get away from my loss, and most people didn't want to hear about my ongoing grief at the loss of "*only"* my dog.

Today, it's three and a half years later. Molly's canine brother, Lex is aging rapidly. His hips are mangled with arthritis and he was just diagnosed with osteosarcoma. But I know what to do now. My experience with Molly taught me that grief is only made greater by not facing it. I know now that life with our canine children is short. We can't fix them when they break, when they are meant to go back to God. But they teach us so much while they are here.

For all that you taught me, my Molly, I'm forever grateful to you.

Just Wait

by Lynn Bukowski

At eleven forty-two pm. on a Wednesday night I open the front door to a weary-eyed social worker, a police officer so rigid he looks to be vibrating, and a two foot tall blanket that may have been light green at some point in its history. I step to the side to allow them entry. No one moves. Red, our Golden Retriever, who is usually attached to my hip, stays in the doorway in a sit position but his front paws creep forward until the tip of his black nose nudges the blanket.

A tiny hand appears, touches the top of Red's head, and then quickly withdraws. The movement snags a silky frayed edge and the cloth falls away to reveal a mess of brown hair, round blue eyes and a perfect spray of freckles across cheeks and nose. The boy stares straight ahead, jaw set, lips rigid, "I not talk," he says.

I nearly smile, but this feels like a test, so I nod once and say, "Good to know." I ignore the woman's raised eyebrows and instead, turn and walk down the hallway, as though welcoming a frightened child and two strangers into my home with five children asleep upstairs and my husband deployed is simply another day in the life. It isn't. But I had trained for and signed on to be an emergency therapeutic foster parent and it is far too late at night to admit I might be in over my head.

A piercing rigid scream coincides with my flipping a switch in the kitchen. The brightness of the room seems to ignite panic in the child and he dissolves onto the floor, skitters across the tile and comes to rest as a steady choking sob in the corner of the room. I glance toward the sound of whispers in the hallway, hear the baby cry, hear the upstairs floor creek with footsteps and nearly miss the words from woman to officer, "I thought I mentioned he doesn't like to be touched."

I focus on the dog huddling peacefully next to the trembling boy in the corner of my kitchen and think: who the hell touched him? Then, I think: the dog is fine, the boy is breathing, the floor is clean.

The floor is clean? Truly, this is my brain in crisis-mode.

I'm sure I hear God chuckle as I usher the adult people out of my home with a quiet thank you. To my ears I sound like a crazed Ms. Manners. I had just barely controlled my urge to laugh aloud at their parting promise that the child would be placed in a permanent foster home by the weekend.

"Also," the social worker turns in the doorway, "James is terrified of men."

"Terrific." I say, noting the pitifully small paper sack in my hand with the name "James" scrawled in black marker. It is weep or deal time so I close the door, find two pillows and a large quilt and settle in for a long night on the kitchen floor.

Until that night I thought I knew what was in the next room, what kids like for dinner, what grass feels like on bare feet. I was comfortable with the orderly mess I orchestrated each day. It was crazy and hard and joyful, and it was mine. Until the night of James - when I discovered that in three years a child can be so badly abused that his small world is reduced to a corner in the kitchen and an old soiled blanket.

On day two, James and I compromise with a makeshift bed upstairs next to Red's pillow at the end of the baby's crib. He dresses himself, but only while underneath the blanket draped over his head. He eats with his hands, brushes his teeth, and appears intrigued by the maneuverings of the older children in the house. They speak to him, answer for him, proclaim his cuteness and ignore his quirks.

Still, he does not talk. He pays no attention to the baby, Aaron (or so I think), who for most of the day remains strapped to my chest in a sling. Until one morning when, in the midst of our normal chaotic breakfast comprised of signing papers, packing lunches, and kid arguments, James tentatively steps very close to me and with the edge of his soiled blanket, reaches up to baby Aaron and wipes at a bit of spittle. For an instant all activity stops. A collective deep breath fills the space and then through the guidance of angels perhaps we all know not to react to this tender moment and chaos resumes as usual.

 Baths were out. Since I drew the line at Red and the blanket in the bathtub, our first attempt at bathing ended in shrill screams and a brief regression to his safe place in the corner. Sheri, our eight year old daughter, cleaned out the plastic baby pool, enlisted Red's patient cooperation, and together with a bar of soap and a three-year old at the end of a hose, we had a semi-clean boy and a sparkling Golden Retriever every other day.

The social worker called two weeks, four days and three hours into James' emergency stay. She was still speaking, her words a distant drone through the phone line - when James came up and took my hand (a touch miracle of its own) pointing with glee to his tiny drawings on the wall in his safe corner. This was the first true smile, the first initiated touch and the first emotion I'd seen from this child. After some confusion, as he still wasn't speaking, I realized he had drawn meticulously neat small dots to represent hours, circles around exactly 24 dots to represent days and squares around each set of circles to represent weeks. Also, he was partial to blue crayons, which oddly complimented my yellow flowered wallpaper.

The social worker had called to notify me of a permanent arrangement for James. I responded simply, "No thanks, he's already home."

Patience is not one of my virtues. I tend to set my course and go, obstacles be damned. James, though, elicited a calm in me I cannot to this day explain. I was content to watch him watch life, soak it in, and return to his safe place in the corner as necessary.

Red was my Godsend and as it turns out, James' confidant. Shortly after the baby pool baths began, and out of necessity, I showed James how to brush Red's coat. Our back deck was about a foot off the ground and built around a large oak tree. Each day, James would sit on the edge of the deck next to the Oak trunk. Red would cuddle up to his left side and as the brushing began, a methodical, tender child stroke. James would quietly talk. Usually, I sat in a glider on the other side of the massive oak rocking Aaron, but James never seemed to notice that there was anyone else in the world except for him and Big Red. He told Red in vivid detail about his broken arms, his round scars, his mommy's bruised eye, how Man #3 was more mean than Man #2, but wrestled better until he got mad. How touching meant hurts and talking was trouble and how he thought maybe Man #1 might be his dad who went to Heaven but mommy didn't tell him for sure.

A month after James came to live with us; Steve called to tell me he was on his way home, having just arrived back on base. Over the phone I told him we now had six children under the roof. "And one more thing," I paused, "reportedly, James has an intense fear of men."

There was complete silence for a moment and then Steve responded with a quiet, "Okay." An hour later he and a teammate, Mike, a 6'4" tank of a man, walked through the front door booming with laughter and the announcement that all kids interested in ice cream had five minutes to show up at the door ready to go. Red, although vibrating with excitement that Dad was home, stayed next to James in the corner of the kitchen, both wide-eyed and silent, save for the dog's thumping tail.

After a quick kiss for me and without fanfare or pretense, Steve approached James, held out his hand and said, "Hey James, I'm Steve and this is Mike. How about we go get some ice cream?" James never spoke, but he held Steve's hand for the entire ice cream outing and returned home sound asleep and slung over Mike's shoulder like a precious ruck sack with Red keeping watch. Apparently, that "intense fear of men" had nothing to do with Navy SEALs.

"Thirty-five days and James only talks to Red. Why won't he speak to any of us?" I wondered aloud over coffee on a rare, quiet Sunday morning.

Steve barely looked up from the paper and said, "He will. Just wait."

On the forty-second day of James, a sunny, breezy day, James asked Red if he ever wanted to be a cowboy one day. I heard hope in the question and I so wished Red could just this once answer the question with a hearty Yes! I was still smiling to myself when I heard Red's sigh from the other side of the Oak, heard his nails scratch the deck board as he stood and shook. James ¨C holding on to Red's collar ¨C appeared at the side of my chair. He reached out and patted Aaron's head, touched my hand and asked, "Could Red and me please have a butter jelly sammich, Mommy Lynn?"

Exactly one year, thirty days and two hours from the first moment we met and I have the wallpaper saved to prove it - James left our home to live with his natural grandparents in another state. I have heard that James learned to ride horses, to be a cowboy, and in high school he began to train dogs specifically to work with abused children.

I learned patience that year from Steve, which is ironic. He epitomized impatience in nearly all matters, unless it counted. He intuitively knew when to act and when to wait. Thus I learned to wait and to listen. Really listen. I learned to listen to small sounds, soothe night terrors, watch small gestures, tiny movements, and to wait with baited breath for the moment when a simple request for a butter jelly sammich rocked my world.

I testified in court to make sure Man #3 saw the inside of a jail cell. I also kept notes: The Journals of James, and wept in the shower each night for the pain this child had endured. Most importantly, perhaps, I let Red take the lead in healing, because he knew more, instinctively, about how to wait than any of us.

We have to be willing to wait.

"No matter how little money and how few possessions you own, having a dog makes you rich."
-- Louis Sabin

Easter Dinner

by Bruce Littlefield

Jasper's stomach, by way of his nose, controls most of his life. One of Jasper's parents was most certainly a beagle, and as anyone who has been owned by anything beagle will tell you, when a beagle's nose talks, every bit of his being listens.

When it comes to food, Jasper is a furry MacGyver too. A few years back we set humane traps to catch a skunk and found them stripped of their marshmallow bait over and over again. We'd set the trap and within hours, it would be empty of both morsel and skunk. This pattern went on for days. Set. Wait. Vanish. We were convinced our skunk was the smartest Pepe Le Pew on the planet.

Finally, in an attempt to at least see the stinker in action, I set the trap and took a bird's eye view from an upstairs window. Within minutes, I witnessed the crime. Jasper sauntered up to the trap, looked right then left, took the rope in his mouth, and proceeded to shake the cage as if he were conquering a wild animal. One by one the marshmallows popped out like candy from his personal piñata, and he happily devoured the treats, ignoring my dramatic tapping on the window.

After that incident, we decided to forgo skunk capture and attempt to blast it out with rock music. It was much better on Jasper's waistline and actually proved to work.

Over the years with Jasper, we were basically in a constant state of trying to outsmart him. We had to secure the trashcan with childproof locks. No food could be left below counter level. He even got around that when the reward was big. One Christmas, in order to claim a cooling Kentucky bourbon pie from the window sill, he figured out how to push a chair across the kitchen, climb atop it and stand on his hind legs. When we came home to find the mess, Jasper was drunk with happiness.

But last Easter morning takes the prize. We were in the car en route to help friends move a sofa bed they were giving away to another friend's house. Scott drove while I munched on a chocolate bunny I'd pulled from my Easter basket. Jasper sat on my lap in the front seat of the car and drooled, having already consumed the treats from his. "Mine," I said authoritatively. "Chocolate bunny bad for Jasper."

The lingering chill in the air left the blooms looking less than inspired, but as Scott, Jasper and I drove down the road we caught a few fleeting glimpses of forsythia yellow and crocus purple. Churches were spilling synthetic color onto their lawns and into the road.

"Watch out!" I shrieked. Scott ground our Jeep to a halt. An errant egg hunter in brightly dyed taffeta had hopped onto the road. The taffeta'd toddler was quickly followed by a woman wearing what looked like bright pink drapes. Her outfit was as horrible as her scream.

"Sorry," she mouthed to us as she toted her toddler back onto the lawn.

I waved to the twosome and pouted to Scott, "I didn't get a cute Easter outfit this year."

"You didn't need one," he said. "We're not going to church, we're going to move a sofa."

Oh yeah. The Serta Perfect Sleeper eagerly unfolded as we (well, Scott and our friend Jim) carried it to their truck. Jim's wife Immy and I followed along behind, picking up errant pillows and trying to keep the movers in line. When we finally got the couch nested neatly on the back of their truck, Immy suggested that we go get lunch at the local diner. Jasper was excited by the mention of lunch. He knew we'd bring him a t-r-e-a-t. (We'd taken to spelling the word because any mention of the word would send Jasper into spasm.)

After lunch, a more full foursome and Jasper (happy with his two fries) headed to deliver the sofa to our friend Lee. Immy and Jim were ahead in their truck; Scott and I were following in the Jeep. At this point, you're probably guessing that something went horribly awry. Did the couch slide off the truck? Nope. Did Scott and Jim crash? No. Did we get pulled over for too wide a load? Nah. The couch delivery actually went off without a glitch¡ save for one minor trouble. Lee's front door had to be removed to get it through, which did take a few extra minutes and tools.

After the successful move, we all stood on the porch, enjoying the early spring air. "Where's Jasper?" I asked.

"Oh, he's exploring," Lee said.

"Believe me," I said assuredly, "if he's not here, he's off finding something to eat." After a few minutes of calling, I got him to come with a sneaky: "Hey Jasper, you want a treat?" He sauntered onto the porch, looking as guilty as a kid who'd been caught with his hand in the cookie jar.

"Where ya been, boy?" Scott asked. After a brief inspection turned up no evidence of wrongdoing, we decided it was time to go. We had one more thing to pick up: a bookshelf for Jim and Immy at the house their daughter Kathy had just sold. We waved our goodbyes, and Jasper lethargically climbed into my lap on the front seat. Halfway to Kathy's, Jasper's stomach kicked like a donkey and before I could get words out of my mouth, the entire contents of Jasper's stomach came out of his into my lap, oozing down my legs, and seeping into my shoes.

"Aaaaaaah!" I convulsed. "Aaaaaaaah!" I was coated in what looked like black coffee grinds and what smelled like poop.

Scott burst into grossed out laughter. "It's not funny!" I cried. "I'm going to throw up. You know I have a weak stomach." My entire family does. My mother often recounts the nauseating story of one Disney vacation in which we drove home in a van full of vomit. My sister's yuke had caused my brother to yuke and that had caused me to yuke. It is a rubber laying, emergency lane rattling memory I'll never forget.

"What should I do?" Scott asked, trying to choke back laughter as I tried to choke down vomit.

"Just drive," I barked.

"Are you okay, Jasper?" Scott cooed sympathetically. "What'd you eat, boy?"

"Whatever it was, it's all out on me," I belched. "Drive faster."

"Emergency!" Scott announced with lights flashing and horn honking as we pulled into Kathy's driveway. "Bruce is covered in throw up."

I stepped out of the car dripping black, poop-smelling granules.

"Ewww," Immy said, scrunching up her nose. "That's Malorganite."

"What's that?"

"You don't want to know."

"Yes, I do."

"No, you don't," she insisted. "It's an organic fertilizer made out of processed human feces."

"Poooooooooooop!" I took off my clothes as I ran down the sidewalk toward Kathy's. house "Find me something to wear, Immy!" Kathy had emptied the house of all her clothes in preparation for her summer renter. As I showered off, I heard Immy scurrying around the house opening doors and slamming drawers, so I knew the outfit was going to be less than perfect.

"Have you found anything, Immy?" I yelled through the crack of the bathroom door.

"Well," she said, "this is all I could find." Her arm came into the bathroom.

"You've got to be kidding." She wasn't. It was literally the only garment in the house, left behind, hanging on the back of a door. It was that or my vomit-covered outfit. I chose that.

I walked out of the house. "Golly!" Jim chuckled. "Nice legs."

"Shut up," I said, angrily sashaying to the car. "Let's go. We can all laugh about this later."

Jim and Immy took off ahead of us with the bookcase, and we pulled out after them. When we turned onto Lucas Avenue, I heard heaving in the backseat. "Pull over!" I told Scott. "He's going to throw up. Pull over right now!" Scott screeched the Jeep to a halt on the side of the road, and I jumped out of the car and opened Jasper's door.

I stood over Jasper, soothingly talking to him as if he were one of my drunk and puking dorm mates in college. A car passed, honking and catcalling. "What are you looking at?" I screamed back at them. "Haven't you ever seen a dog barf?!" Suddenly, in one horrifying moment I realized that what they were looking at was me in my Easter outfit¡ a pink satin Victoria's Secret negligee, hitting my thighs like a Tina Turner mini-skirt.

I'd like to say that we all learned a lesson that day. I certainly learned that in the future I might be careful what I wish for. Or at least more specific. Jasper, however, had learned nothing and his stomach recovered quickly. That night, at Jim and Immy's Easter dinner, we all gasped as Jasper walked across the room carrying the entire Easter ham in his mouth.

Remembering Luis: Fields of Barley, Fields of Gold

by Joanna Perry-Folino

It's been nearly one year since my small white Havanese dog, Luis, left the world, released back into the natural order of stars and atoms and energy. I sleep with his photo and a little cedar box of his ashes next to my bed. And at least once a week, before oblivion settles over me, I look at his photo and remember what it was like to be unconditionally loved and to unconditionally love back.

My ex, who probably was always a little jealous of my adoration of this creature, gave me a gift the other day, a book of stories by famous writers called Dog Is My Co-Pilot, subtitled "Great Writers on the World's Oldest Friendship" from the editors of The Bark, a newsletter about dogs. I opened it tentatively because I was fearful of the words inside breaking me open again to the agony of the loss of a companion who could only speak to me through his eyes, his touch and his childlike sounds. Maybe that's exactly why we got on so well. No words ever got in our way.

Having experienced many other recent losses in my life including two miscarriages, a father taken bit by bit by Alzheimer's, the splintering of my birth family into factions, a supportive friend of 15 years whose body and life was destroyed by Lou Gehrig's disease and the premature death of my brother-in-law from leukemia, I wondered if being a voyeur into other people's relationships with canines was a good idea for someone who was trying her best to move on. But I opened the cover despite my fears and jumped into the doggy dish.

Erica Jong, the first writer I encountered, states that a dog is a woman's best friend. "Like men, dogs think with their noses. Unlike men, dogs are fiercely loyal," Jong says. Yes, probably true most of the time, although I'd like to believe there are men out there who could be fiercely loyal to their women. I'd like to believe it, although more often than not, what proves true is that when men are the least bit insecure or feeling neglected or unloved or not satisfied sexually, they will sleep with other women and lie about it. We all know this happens, and we know women do the same thing, though probably less often. We are all of us, men and women, only human. We're not dogs. We haven't yet evolved emotionally to that place.

This is exactly what makes dogs so remarkable. Why they've been our companions for so many centuries and why women are now seeing how great and powerful their relationship with canines can be, unlike anything they will ever experience. Anyone out there who has a dog companion knows exactly what I mean.

I'm going to be brave here and tell you exactly what I fear about my dating life now that I'm over 50. I'm terrified there's no one out there for me. No one who can put up with my nuttiness, my anxieties, my insecurities, my moodiness. No one who will see the inside of me and still love me fiercely. No one who will ever again love me like Luis did. There, it's out there. And now that I've said it, I feel better. This is the kind of thing I would tell Luis. He always listened and reassured me that it was just not the case. After all, he certainly loved me in all my horrifying neediness and with all my "stuff," right?

Now that I think about it, I've already experienced what some people never experience in any relationship of any kind. When Luis died, I understood, for example, that I could cope with devastating loss. He taught me (and Jong reminds me) that when you love a creature, dog or human, you can "pick up its shit and not mind... that nothing is disgusting in love -- neither smells nor spills." Most importantly, I saw that I really could hang in there, be fully present, right up until the last devastating moment. I learned I won't run from the room screaming, but will hold my beloved in my arms and watch the last shudder of his fragile body while tears flood everything in the universe. This is love, isn't it?

After finishing the book, I decided I would discover and commit to another dog companion in a few months. And yes, I'll also keep dating. If a human shows up who's fiercely loyal and finds nothing about me disgusting, neither smells nor spills and I, too, find nothing disgusting about him and can pick up his shit and not mind... well. I'll be in a Sting song... running through fields of barley. Running with Mr. Dog and Mr. Human.

Don't get me wrong. No new dog and no human will ever replace Luis. But according to Jong, "love of a new dog expands the heart." I can hear mine, creaky old thing that it is, stretching every day. And Mr. Whoever You May or May Not Be? You need to know I may never love another like I loved this creature, but such knowledge will be, according to Ms. Erica Jong, and I paraphrase a bit "as sacred to you as God is to prayers."

Thanks dear, sweet wonderful dog of my heart. This is my love song to you, out there running in fields of gold. Ruff ruff.

Vanished in Nepal: an excerpt

by Jit Bahadur Masrangi Magar

A Nepalese army helicopter had shuttled all of us: concerned family members, Sherpas, search dogs, and me¡ up into the Langtang Valley that stretches along the Nepalese-Tibetan border. The old and rusty Alouette needed three flights to complete the trip from Kathmandu to the village of Kyangjing Gompa. The Yangri Khola Gorge. Soon it would become a kind of nemesis for me. My dogs and I would find ourselves here over and over again in the following twenty years of search and rescue missions with SAR Dogs Nepal. We would have great successes and meet great failures. We would save lives and mourn them. We would learn again and again what we already knew: one should never trek alone in the mighty Himalayas!

Three weeks before, on the 7th of June 1990, a foreign trekker from Belgium had gone missing from right about here. He had decided to continue his trek alone after discharging the local guide who had shown him the way from Kyangjing Gompa to the "Ganja La" pass. Our seven member search party along with my two German shepherd tracker dogs was now following exactly the same trail as our missing man. We had already crossed the pass at an altitude of 5200 meters into Helambu, which is the closest popular trekking route north of Kathmandu Valley.

Our first night-camp was nestled between thick patches of long yellowish grass in front of the dark gray rock face below the 5844 meters measuring Naya Kanga peak. The next day in the early morning, our four Sherpa guides had made a brief prayer ceremony. They burned aromatic herbs and juniper twigs as an offering to the mountain spirits and local deities. After that, they served breakfast with biscuits and salted butter tea. At each of the small streams the Sherpas stopped and made their prayer gestures with folded hands before continuing to wade through the ice-cold waters. One of the two Sherpas who accompanied me explained that each stream is considered to be a living water spirit. While crossing a water body like a creek or rivulet one must appease her by saying a certain prayer.

Later that day, we decided to split into two search groups. My tracker dog Eiko stared at the point where his daughter, the man-trailer Britta, disappeared along with the other people. Maybe he expected that they all would re-appear. After a long, quiet moment, Eiko looked up at me, trying to read my body language, perhaps hoping that this was just another training session and that we might soon follow the others to re-unite. But then he seemed to understand and made a single little sound; one of the high pitched whimpers that he would make when he was worried. And then he got down to business.

For hours of searching afterward, men and dog could only talk a sort of sign language with our hands. A verbal conversation was not possible because the Yangri Khola roared like a jet engine. That was OK for me and Eiko: we always spoke without words. Lianas and lichens were growing between branches of trees. Emerging thickly out of the moist saturated air and steaming fog they looked like the long grey-green beards of giant monsters. Our clothes and our luggage were soon soaked with spray droplets from the steaming river. Eiko's fur looked shiny like a silver coat made of chain mail. Wet and dripping, he appeared much thinner, like a starving wolf. He had long given up shaking the water out of his fur. Many times I pulled fat black and brown leeches out of his ears and between his toes. The day was long and so far fruitless.

Then, all of a sudden, Eiko made a discovery: he scratched with his paws and pointed his nose at a small shiny object wedged between pebbles at the riverside. It was a tiny open envelope that was made of aluminum paper and looked almost new. It had once contained ORS, the oral rehydration salt used to make a drink to help the drinker retain electrolyte balance. Its surface was bilingually printed in both Flemish and French and ended with the words "Made in Belgium"! Eiko's extraordinary find proved to me that our missing trekker must have come down this way not so long ago.

What a moment of satisfaction it was for me when my companion found this bit of evidence! Our training and our comradeship were beginning to pay off. I deeply hoped that the man we were searching would be found alive. I hoped to be able to tell to his fiance, who had funded the search, that her premonition was wrong. She had made up her mind to face his death during her very first surveillance flight when she saw beneath her a glistering and foaming wild river winding its way down inside a green jungle belt, embedded in shiny black rock-walls as high as sky grabbers topped with jagged spikes and capped with layers of snow. Anyone attempting to climb out of the gorge would have to conquer those rocks; one would need high tech gear and the skills of an experienced rock climber to do it. And there was not a single trace of any settlement around or inside the area. Furthermore, the gorge was essentially closed at the lower end. There seemed to be only a powerful waterfall as outlet into the open cultivated valley of eastern Helambu.

The only possible way out would be to retreat back up to the Ganja La Pass again. We ourselves, with all our gear and experience, couldn't do it all on foot. So to save time, we decided to be dropped further back up the pass by helicopter into a small open valley the size of a soccer field, a likely place to look for the missing man. Locals in Tarkeghyang knew the place as "Tsetang". Nobody had noticed this spot during previous helicopter flights. Fog or clouds must have veiled the valley from sight before this. The missing trekker's relatives had paid in advance for the army helicopter's reservation for our next trip. It would take us to where we needed to go and assist us by dropping food supplies if it was necessary to extend the search for another week or more.

My team's second journey into the Yangri Khola gorge took place three days later. Early morning on day thirty-two of the trekker's disappearance, Eiko and I arrived by taxi at the office of the Royal Nepalese Air Force' 11th brigade Helicopter Wing near the Kathmandu Domestic Airport. A security guard at the entry gate helped me to unload the taxi. Eiko was inside a transport box and when we lifted the box from the back seat the guard stopped and rang up for permission to let my companion into the military area. I released Eiko from the box and went with him to the "Briefing Room" for the pilots. Inside, there was a set of plain wooden benches that looked both unstable and shabby. Sitting on one of these benches were my two new friends Bom Bahadur and Mingma Sherpa from the Asian Trekking PLTD Agency.

They each gave a broad smile and nod, and then reached out to pet Eiko, who smiled back at them, thumping his tail. Good friends! Between their legs, Mingma and Bom Bahadur were holding backpacks out of which stuck ice axes with coils of ropes attached. We would need all the gear we could safely carry to track and find the missing man. From inside the briefing room a smoky voice finally called out: "Come on in, you guys"! There was a large desk in the center of the room, and the surrounding walls were covered fully in ochre-coloured military maps with red and black number codes showing all parts of Nepal. We were told to sit on another old bench at the side of the room. Eiko settled on the dirt floor beside us. The two pilots in military garb turned their backs on us without looking in our direction when we entered the space. They were studying maps on the table and making marks with a sort of long pencil. Another man was sitting behind the desk and did not make eye contact either.

When finally they decided to look at us they seemed shocked to see a dog in the room...but not shocked in a negative way. "Ah, look what we got here!" said the man behind the desk. "Holy shit, isn't this the real stuff! What the heck is the meaning of this? Can he also fly a helicopter"? Eiko was a powerful and very handsome German shepherd. Most Nepalese knew Alsatian dogs only from photographs and as service dogs of Police and Army. German Shepherds were not seen much outside the

National Police Training Centre in Kathmandu. But the Nepalese King Birendra was also known to have about six of them inside his Royal Palace...so the pilots became very excited when they saw Eiko. They began to pepper me with a lot of questions about my friend, about what kind of tricks he could do and so on. But before I could answer that Eiko was a working trekker worthy of their respect and not a performing animal, we were interrupted by a loud shout from outside.

The guard at the gate was standing in alert mode with his right hand at his cap. A military jeep drove through and stopped in front of our little building. This was my first, and indeed my last, encounter with General Malla, Chief in charge of the 11th Brigade Helicopter Wing. The pilots sprang to attention and saluted him. Above us, a monkey appeared on the roof of the nearby hangar. The smart simian copied the soldier at the gate and saluted the General too. Malla stopped, turned towards the animal and shouted, "At ease, Sergeant Bobo!" The monkey relaxed and showed a broad grin with an ugly set of teeth...then raised his snaky arm to snatch a treat that the General threw to him.

As he walked in, The General turned directly to me and said, solemnly: "So, you are looking for the missing Belgian man? I sincerely hope you will find him. We are pleased to be at your service. Today you and your team will be flying with Captain K.B.Shahi."

One of the three pilots who were standing at attention before us stretched his body to full length and exclaimed "Yessssir! Ready Sssir"! but at the same time his face turned bright red and with his eyes very wide he addressed me, saying: "But, of course, no dog in my aircraft, Mister"!

There was a tense moment of silence in the office. It seemed as if everyone was holding his breath. I could not even find the words to reply to this absurd command. After waiting for an answer from me that did not come the pilot continued, saying gruffly: "I have no problems with you or these two Sherpas. But when this animal panics during flight, as he surely will, we will have to abort the mission. Such a large beast should not be inside a moving helicopter, and you know it"!

"Relax, Captain!" answered General Malla. "How can you not know that the dog is what this mission is all about? A man on a search and rescue trek brings with him no frightened cur, but a dog of calm and skill and ability. He," and here he nodded respectfully at Eiko who looked attentively back, "is the real trekker of the bunch. You have heard the order and you will take them, men and animal all, to the place where they need to go"!

General Malla seemed to be a nice man. He placed real value on the skill and dedication of our team and of my dog companion. Unfortunately, he died some years later in a helicopter crash in the hilly region of Gorkha while on a surveillance flight. Malla's own German shepherd, Bilbo of Bagmati Springs, survived the crash unhurt. Bilbo was an offspring of my dog Eiko, something that General Malla had somehow learned before our encounter that day. No wonder he defended Eiko's role on our search team! He knew who he was dealing with, and what Eiko might be capable of.

And he was not wrong, not wrong at all, in his thinking...

MeiMei

by Alan Paul

I spent well over a year looking for a rescue dog, scouring Petfinder and other websites for hours searching for a friendly dog that didn't shed, a necessity because of my wife Becky's allergies. I quickly learned to moderate my excitement over apparent finds – these sites don't update that often so many of the pets I discovered were already long gone. But I kept looking, kept inquiring, and expanded my search to breed-specific rescue organizations for Tibetan Terriers, Wheaton Terriers, and Labradoodles.

I thought I had found my perfect dog in South Jersey, about an hour from my house. "Arf" sounded great, a poodle mix who was friendly, didn't shed, was great with kids and had been brought to the organization by a woman who had not mistreated the dog but couldn't give him a proper home.

My in-laws were visiting and I asked them to come along. With my wife working, I thought another adult voice of reason would be welcome. I told my mother-in-law Ruth not to let me do anything rash.

Arf was a lovely dog, with sores on his back legs from sleeping on a concrete floor. My kids, then 8, 10 and 13, could handle him, walking him all around the yard and lying down to cuddle him. I did a quick phone consult with Becky who told me to go with my gut, and told the lady we wanted him, asking what we had to do next.

"I think we're all set," she said. "We checked your references. Leah said that you have taken care of her dogs and she will take care of yours, so you won't need a kennel."

"Yep," I replied, impressed that my friend Leah had thought of that on her own. It seemed an excellent payback for having cared for her two sweet, aged Labs.

"That's not realistic," my mother-in-law said. "You're going to need to use a kennel now and then,"

"Nope," I replied, shooting her a look that I hoped said something nicer than "Shut Up!" but firmer than "Huh?"

"It's all set," I insisted. "We took care of Leah's dogs and she will take care of ours."

Ruth wouldn't hear of it: "Oh, the way you travel you are going to have to use a kennel now and then!"

The rescue woman was growing uneasy. "Is this true?" she asked, turning towards me. "We can't have a dog kept in a kennel."

My three kids were sprawled on the gravel driveway canoodling with Arf just 20 feet away as we spoke. I thought that this should be enough of a reference, but I could feel the whole thing slipping away, and Ruth was just getting started. She has a beautiful Airedale named Ava, who is their sixth daughter and now the queen of the house. They bake her biscuits, cook her chicken, and feed her ice cream. She was in a kennel at that very moment. Ruth was not going to accept this insult.

"What's wrong with kennels?" she demanded. "My dog is in a kennel right now. She's with just a few other dogs and they play outside most of the day."

"Well," the woman replied. "That's very lucky for you. But most kennels keep dogs locked up 23 hours a day in cages."

"It doesn't matter!" I said, desperately trying to steer the conversation back to Arf. Back to us. Back to my adorable, loving kids practically making out with the dog just a few feet away. "Kennels don't concern us – because Leah will be taking care of our dog!"

Everyone drifted apart and I went back to my kids and Arf and took further stock of him. He was raggedy but lovable, probably 40 pounds and in need of a little fattening up. They called him a golden doodle but he could have been anything. He looked so happy for this attention and for a moment I contemplated throwing him in the back seat of my minivan and gunning the gas.

My thoughts were interrupted by the return of the dog woman. She was frantic.

"You indicated on your application that your backyard was fenced, but your mother-in-law said that it's not completely secure. Is that true?"

"Well... Yes," I stammered. "It's three-quarters fenced. We haven't had a need for a complete fencing in. But the plan has always been to finish it when we get the dog."

This was all true, but then I uttered the naïve line that sealed my fate: "Maybe we'll just get an invisible fence."

"Oh no! Those are electric fences!"

I quickly stammered that I didn't know that and we wouldn't get one, but Ruth wasn't going to let this insult sit either; they had an invisible fence and no one was going to impugn her love for Ava or imply that she might harm her beloved dog.

"What's the matter with invisible fences? We have one."

"They are electric fences and dogs can be badly shocked or even killed by them!"

I was watching immovable object hit irresistible force and I knew that the only thing truly being damaged was my family's chance of taking Arf home. We parted with assurances that we would hear within a day and that things looked good, but I knew it was over.

That night Becky told me to email and apologize for her mother, but I resisted. She had behaved inappropriately but I agreed with her on every substantive issue - and none of it impacted our ability to care for a dog. "Who cares," my practical wife counseled. "If you want Arf, just do it."

So I did, and it seemed to work. "Thanks for letting me know," read the reply. "You did seem to have different ideas. We will let you know soon."

Then the kicker: "Every family ends up with the dog that they should have."

I knew this was rejection and it filled me with anger. I wanted Arf. My kids wanted Arf. We would provide him with a great home. These rescue people are crazy, I thought. I had already missed out on another dog because I filled out an application honestly, stating that I didn't have a vet for a reference. That disqualified me, which just seemed insane. Why should a person without a pet have a vet? Don't you get the animal first?

It pains me a little to say that the rescue lady was right. We ended up with the dog we should have. It wasn't Arf. It wasn't anything I ever thought I would fall for. It was MeiMei, a seven-pound mixed breed terrier with one ear up and one ear down who looks rather like an alien teddy bear, a castoff from Lilo and Stitch.

Months went by after the Arf fiasco. I continued to scour the Internet and after several more false hopes, I finally gave up on finding a rescue dog. Against every belief I hold, I started looking at breeders' sites. I spoke to goldendoodle people and labradoodle folks. I admired Portuguese Water Dogs but feared their size and energy and broke down and agreed to consider a cockapoo at my daughter's urging. They looked very cute but the name was a barrier. Couldn't they have come up with something other than COCK-a-POO?

Then we went to Michigan to visit my wife's family and spent days with Ava and my sister-in-law's little schnoodle Oscar. He's a lovely thing, a furry, cuddly little ball of love. When we got back to New Jersey, Eli, my then 11-year-old son, said, "Let's go to the pound one more time tomorrow."

We had been going to our local no-kill shelter for months but had given up. Too many hounds, too few shedless dogs. We walked in the next morning and saw the usual array of snarling Pit Bull mixes and lovely mixed-breed hounds that wouldn't work for us. Then we walked into the back room. It stank of piss and shit. There were cages everywhere. Dogs growling and barking. And on top of a big cage sat a little cage. Inside the little cage sat a tiny little moppet. "Look at that one," said 8-year-old Anna.

I looked. I saw. I fell in love. This poor little thing looked terrified. She weighed less than 7 pounds. Her eyes were covered in black gunk, but peering though the schmutz were soulful little dark orbs, and they were pleading. They were saying, "Take me, please."

I had never in my life considered having such a tiny dog. I grew up with a golden retriever and I always admired big Frisbee-catching mutts. My wife wanted a dog that would run with her. We'd always made fun of little yappy dogs like this little thing the shelter had tagged Tinkerbell.

All that went out the window in a second because of the way she was looking at me. This dog had soul. I had been looking long enough to be pretty sure that she wouldn't shed. I asked if we could take her for a walk. Someone got us a leash and off we went.

She was as sweet as she appeared to be, thrilled to get out of that cage, and anxious to get outside, away from the big dogs who seemed to terrify her. She was easy for the kids to control. We walked around and we sat and played. This dog was lively, friendly, cute, loving – and reeking of a sad desperation for a new life.

I told the kids she looked good, as we gave her back and headed home. I already felt certain she was the dog for us, but I didn't want my kids to be disappointed again. I said we had to discuss it with mom, and in any case Tinkerbell couldn't be adopted for another week, having been found in a nearby park. Local finds had to stay in the shelter for 7 days before they could be adopted.

The next day I returned alone. I wanted to make a rational decision, not an emotional one fueled by the kids. As soon as I walked into the room, Tinkerbell jumped up, eyes alight, tail wagging. She recognized me! I took her for a walk again and this time I sat down in a chair and put her in my lap. She curled up in a ball and looked up at me with her lovely, gunk-caked eyes. I held her for a good half hour communing, but also wanting to make sure that she didn't shed. We got up to go inside and there was no sign of fur on me.

It broke my heart to hand her back and watch her be returned to the little cage. I went home, thinking about this little dog constantly. In the morning, as soon as the kids went to school, I returned and signed her out as a foster dog. Even if someone showed up to claim her, I wanted to give her the gift of freedom from that cage. I wanted to get her away from the big snarling dogs, give her a bath, get her eyes cleaned up, see how she was in our house to make sure Becky wasn't allergic. I wanted to see if she was as lovely as she appeared to be.

She was. I counted down the four days until we could adopt her and praying that no one showed up to claim her. On day four, the phone rang I was sitting on the couch, with the dog we had renamed MeiMei – little sister in mandarin – sitting on my lap. Anna was next to me, petting the dog's head. It was someone from the pound.

"Do you want Tinkerbell or not?" I was brusquely asked. "Five people are lined up for her from our web posting."

"They can't have her," I replied, alarmed at the thought that this was even possible. Anna let out a loud cheer.

Two years earlier my family had returned from living in China for four years. MeiMei means little sister, a crucial word in Chinese culture that applies to the youngest female in a household. MeiMei was one of us. No one ever doubted her full family membership from the moment we brought her home. About six weeks later, Becky had surgery on her leg and was bedridden for a week. MeiMei didn't leave her side, growling at any non-family member who approached. Her devotion and loyalty could never be doubted.

And neither could ours to her. She sleeps at our feet, wakes up Anna every morning with a lick to the cheek, growls at any stranger who approaches our abode, ready to throw her seven pounds in front of any perceived threat to my family – her family - protecting us as if her life depended on it. The feeling is mutual.

Cookie

by Julie Poland

We thought we knew what we were getting into when we adopted Cookie. We were dog owners before, and dealt with the house training, the mouthing, the grooming, the walking, etc. We had a preschooler who LOVED our first dog, Chester, and she knew how to give commands and deliver reward biscuits properly from her chubby hands. But we had never had a Lab.

It was winter and there was snow on the ground when we visited the farm where Cookie was being raised with her littermates. You probably think we must have been nuts to consider housetraining a puppy in the middle of the coldest part of the year. But our daughter was mourning the loss of her canine best friend – as were we. This was not a rational decision, but rather an emotional one.

The owner of the farm took us into the kitchen, and then went into another room. All of a sudden a stampede of brown Lab puppies pounded into the kitchen. The leader of the mini-pack had the most beautiful amber-colored eyes. They reminded me of my beloved Chester. I was done in as of that minute; this little girl doggy was going to be mine. Did I say that my husband and daughter were there too?

We named her Cookie because she looked like a chocolate cookie. And it seemed that she grew in one or two afternoons while we sat watching her play on the floor with our little girl. We had a crate from our other pets, and Cookie outgrew it in only a couple of weeks. We borrowed a larger crate from our friends, and she outgrew that one too in short order. Finally we purchased a crate that was so big that our four and-a-half year old could climb inside with her.

Cookie loved everybody – and still does. She was so energetic that her chases with the cats around the first floor of our house left serious grooves in the old pine floors. She wiped out quite a few times when the throw rugs in the kitchen didn't accommodate her galloping and rather uncoordinated cornering. And she baptized herself in the goldfish pond out back within twenty-four hours of coming to our house.

After having a dog that had a very short cropped tail, we were surprised at the amount of strength and velocity a Labrador's tail could generate. We cleared the coffee tables for good after Cookie cleared them the first couple of times with her vigorous wagging.

We had to be careful about where we stood when we greeted her, because her tail thwacking the wall could wake our daughter from a sound sleep.

Cookie and our daughter's impending school years were the catalysts for our moving to a bigger space with a yard. We loved our city house and the character that we had so lovingly built into it with every choice we made during its rehab. We shed a few tears when we said goodbye. But our daughter was approaching her fifth birthday and Cookie her sixth month when we moved into our next house.

This place was new construction, and there was no trace of grass on the yard when we moved in, so Cookie and I walked endless laps around the neighborhood. Some of our mileage was so she could accomplish her dogly duties outdoors, but a lot of it was to help her work off some of her seemingly boundless Lab energy. She went to the bus stop with us every morning, and greeted each child and parent at the corner with an attempted lick on the nose. Sometimes she succeeded when we weren't quick enough with the leash.

My aging parents weren't accustomed to such a big dog. Cookie almost knocked my mother over with her all-paws-on-deck greeting, and she had a habit of goosing my father, which he found irritating. But both of her "grandparents" understood her rambunctiousness as affection, and they learned to deal with it.

Our hopes of letting Cookie run around our now grown-in grass led us to install a radio fence around the perimeter of our property. There was a big problem, however. Our dear doggie found almost anyone worth being zapped in the collar to greet. The neighbors across the street, owners of a very dear Golden Retriever, had the same brand of fence as ours, operating at the same frequency. Cookie would get zapped going out of our yard, into theirs, back out of theirs, and back into ours. She seemed immune to the supposed training effect.

One day she exited our yard through the invisible fence because she saw another dog outside in the block behind us. The other dog's owner called her dog inside, and Cookie followed the dog into the other owner's house, racing down the center hall and bouncing off the couch cushions in their family room in her excitement. Red-faced, we escorted her home.

Ultimately we inadvertently cut the wire in several places during our various landscaping projects, so we gave up on ever having our Lab hanging out in the yard. Instead, we committed to give her at least one 20-30-minute walk per day so she can exercise her legs and her nose.

When Cookie was about four, we adopted a second child. Our new daughter came home as a toddler, and Cookie would lie completely flat on the floor for the baby to play with her. Our little girl ran her kiddy car over Cookie's tail, tried to ride her, and covered Cookie with stuffed animals while she relaxed on the couch. That sweet dog just gazed with loving eyes at the little girl with the devilish twinkle in hers.

Cookie is now more than ninety in doggie years, and arthritis and hip dysplasia are catching up with her. We let her take the lead in deciding where we are going to walk on most days. We've had to shorten our route to accommodate her stiffness, and sometimes we have to help her jump up on our bed at night because she can't do it on her own any more. She mostly stays in one spot during the day, lying on the carpet directly in front of the door so any person entering or exiting the house has to squeeze through an impossibly narrow crack.

We're not sure how long our Cookster is going to be able to be with us. But we are

still happy when she sees another dog or a stray cat and starts to do her boinga boinga bouncy routine. We ply her with extra treats, and we give her fish oil and glucosamine to try to help her be comfortable. Our younger daughter asks us sometimes what kind of dog we're going to get next. But we aren't ready to discuss that. We love our Cookie, and we're going to enjoy every moment we have with her.

Cookie enjoying special time with our youngest, Allison, and all her fuzzy friends

Missing Bud

by Mike Ritland

The first time I laid eyes on him, on his shiny clean black coat and piercing blue eyes, I realized I would be involved with dogs for the rest of my life.

He was the first dog I'd had the pleasure of having as my very own; a black lab puppy, 7 weeks old, brought home by my parents when I was just a boy. My brothers and sisters and I had been bugging them for years to get us a dog, and finally they decided to bless us with this one. It was one of the happiest days I can remember, although I couldn't truly know what an impact it would have on my rest of life.

We named him Bud.

Just like all puppies, Bud was all over the place and into just about everything. Even at an early age, however, he was a very quick learner. Now, none of us were exactly skilled in training dogs at that time, but it didn't take long to figure out that he would offer shapeable behaviors to us, that we could condition him to behave just by using food that he was crazy for. Our whole family realized the power of positive reinforcement and operant conditioning when we used popcorn (!) to reinforce basic obedience with him. He ultimately became a well behaved dog with very few exceptions. Although, like all dogs, he would take advantage of those exceptions for an easy score if the timing was just right!

Bud meant the world to me. And by that I mean that he was my closest ally every day, rain or shine. There isn't an aspect of my childhood that doesn't include him. I took him for several hour-long walks each day after school just because I enjoyed spending one-on-one time with him so much. On weekends, my dad and I would take him over to the local golf course, spending hours watching him run, hunt and chase small game. I had never before understood the extent to which dogs relied on their inherited genetics, but as I watched Bud use wind in conjunction with his nose to find the smallest of things to consume, his innate ability to use odor to hunt and scavenge was apparent to me. That's one of the things that I found, and still find, most intriguing about dogs. I would see Bud do it time and time again, and somehow I was impressed with every find.

The genetics of this particular dog, however, were not what was what made Bud so special to me. The bond, trust, and relationship that he and I shared were what mattered. Not a day went by when we didn't spend time together. Sometimes we would lie on the floor side by side. Sometimes we would play ball. Sometimes I would just tell him about my day. No matter what, he always "looked" at me. His eyes said exactly what I needed to hear, and he taught me about what it meant to be loyal. He had the ability to make bad days bearable, good days better, and great days seared into my mind as childhood memories that will always hold a special place in my heart.

It's funny sometimes to think that no matter how many dogs I have had the pleasure of spending time with, in so many different capacities, it's memories of Bud that still remind me why I do what I do for a living. If not for my first dog and our bond, I would not be who I am or where I am now. He left an unmistakable mark on me. Bud is still the model for what I continue to look for in a dog today.

So here's to you, Bud dog. Thanks for teaching me so much more than I could ever have taught you. May the squirrels and rabbits be aplenty over the rainbow bridge. May we take long walks together again.

I still miss you, buddy.

Mike Ritland

"I've seen a look in dogs' eyes, a quickly vanishing look of amazed contempt, and I am convinced that basically dogs think humans are nuts."

- John Steinbeck

The One Day Dog

by George White

As I grew up, my parents never sat me down and had the talk with me. Several times I would think it was coming I'd hear a whisper in a hall, or see them huddled over a cup of Mormon-friendly PostumPostum, I'd linger a bit in anticipation of getting the talk, but after a few minutes of me standing there not speaking it just got awkward, so I'd shuffle off, mumbling I'll just be in my room if you need me, or something equally hopeful. They would have smelled my desperation if Jovan musk wasn't so cheap and sold in walking-distance malls.

Son, owning a dog is a big responsibility. It's a huge metaphor for life. You have to feed it like it's your very soul. You are ultimately responsible for the happiness and well-being of another spirit. A Blithe Spirit, to use a term you might find comfortable, since you seem to like being in those drama productions at your school that we never come to a spirit of which you and you alone are totally in charge. They must be walked, and you must pick up their shit on the lawn like you love it. If we ever step in the unpicked-up shit, we will beat you like a red-headed stepchild. If you think you are ready to own and care for a dog, we can form a little committee and once you and your three brothers have all decided on one type of dog, we will go buy one.

The same dog?! We couldn't have decided on the same pizza, let alone a dog. I realized that I couldn't swap a poodle for a German Shepherd like it was Halloween candy, so I just kept relatively quiet. We never did that family outing where we walked up and down the aisles of the SPCA. I know how it goes everyone is looking for a puppy. There's a crowd around the pen with the mass of wiggling yellow fur, and tiny children are being licked by a young pup named I want this one daddy!

But I keep walking, and notice a lone, older dog in a pen that no one cared to clean today. She has one ear sticking up. She shakes a little as I walk in, because she isn't used to visitors and doesn't want to get her hopes up again. Life doesn't throw a tennis ball at every dog. She creaks up with hesitation and early hip dysplasia like a girl at the very end of the prom who's finally asked to dance. There's something in this dogs eyes that look back into mine, and start telling me her story. I want to hear more, so I take sign the papers, and I take her home.

After months of slow bonding and endless trips to the vet to try to heal everything that probably got her abandoned in the first place, we are in love. Our slow-mo montage is laid on top of a Maroon 5 ballad, where we romp through fields. We sit in front of the roaring fireplace in our mountain chalet, and I take a quick minute to look up from my novel and smile at the sight of her sleeping all curled up, wondering why that doesn't hurt her back and how I ever lived without her.

Yeah, I never had that.

Like many people, my Aunt Cathie loves her dogs. She has passed this love sweetly to my cousin Sean, and it's heartwarming to watch their hearts melt at even the thought of their animals. Cathie got this gift from her mother, who we called Baby. Baby once had a black lab, Joker, who was able to jump her six-foot fence and run away. His desire to fly to freedom made no sense to me, because Baby's home and loving care were what all people, not just dogs, should have wanted to jump into.

Her son-in-law, my Uncle Jim, was playing golf one day. His caddy, James, happened to live in Baby's detached guest house over the garage. In addition to shining golf shoes and recommending a three iron over a five, he would help Baby with stuff around the house. One day, as James handed Jim his driver, his hand lingered on the club, not letting go. Mr. Jim, there's a dog in your mother-in-law's yard dragging around a skillet tied to his neck. Jim appreciated the nerve it took James to speak to him about this deep concern. Smiling, he explained it all as he swung: That's just to keep him from jumping over the fence.

Yes, exhausted and frustrated from hunting and searching and dragging crazy Joker back into the compound, Baby had grabbed a cast-iron skillet from the kitchen she never cooked in, and tied it to a long chain attached to Joker's collar. He could walk around the yard, dragging the huge, heavy, chicken-frying skillet but he couldn't jump over the fence. He never figured out why he couldn't jump, he just accepted it and roamed the grounds semi-freely. Occasionally his chain would get caught up on a tree trunk or a car tire, but he'd sit, patiently waiting for someone to pass by and hear his eyes pleading, Be a lamb and untangle me.

My cousin Sean and I later used this idea to attach our monkey to a cable between two trees in our yard on Balboa Island. He could zip-zip back and forth, and was still hands-free to touch things incessantly, but unable to run away with our $3500.

I got the itch for a dog years ago in Los Angeles. I decided to scratch it on a Jack Russell terrier. I found a farm in Thousand Oaks that also bred champion thoroughbred horses, and drove out on a beautiful sunny Sunday to just have a little look. Los Angeles is full of canyons and valleys with properties that even Will Rogers would still be discovering, so I was thrilled but not surprised to drive into this never-before-imagined farm.

A Hallmark commercial, starring me, began rolling: As I parked and walked toward the huge, stereotypical red barn, a dozen Jack Russell tiny, fat puppies bounded out and ran down the expansive, rolling green lawn. One particular puppy leaped right into my sucker-arms. I wrote the check, tucked the pup in the passenger seat and drove off onto the Sunset. Boulevard.

Once home, I fussed over him and played with him. I took Sam, his new name, to a dinner party that night with David Youse and Tai Babilonia, passing him around like an hors d'oeurve. Later, I pulled him into bed with me, now not alone for once in a very long time. We clung together all night, each sniffing the other and asking ourselves what we had gotten into.

Before I hesitantly went to work the next day, I left his food and water in my bedroom, near the bathroom floor, thinking this would be the easiest place to clean up the inevitable pee. I spoke in a loving, hopeful, sing-song voice as I showed all this to him, left a gay-crazy amount of toys piled up, and closed the door gently.

It was dark when I got home. I didn't know yet to leave a light on for him. I eased open the front door to prevent his excited little body from squirming out past the guy he barely knew and might not remember.

But he wasn't waiting. Panicked, I flipped on the lights and started searching the house, sure that he had escaped out a door I left open or had been robbed by a PETA rogue. I hadn't even had the chance to act non-repulsed by the saliva-covered tennis ball I hadn't even yet had the chance to throw over and over and over.

When I walked in my bedroom, there he was, huddled in the exact same spot I had placed him in near his untouched food. He hadn't even chewed the price tags off the toys, nor drank any water. In a second I realized that the bouncing puppy I had watched run down the huge, rolling lawn, and had fallen so quickly in love with, was in shock and missed that farm and the horses. I had made a mistake asking him to accept my life.

I called the farm and told the owner what I felt. She understood. I drove him back to the farm immediately, and even in the dark, he ran out of my car, up the giant lawn and into the dark barn. I hope he has had a wonderful life, and not thought for a moment of selfish me.

All of the time I get is borrowed. Of all my travels, I have marveled most at the fantastic, shockingly pristine beauty of Alaska, which is rivaled by nothing in the world except the love I saw bestowed on the Alaskan sled dogs by their owners. Seeing Alaska, even alone, is as breathtaking as visiting Paris in love.

Twice I've helicoptered up through a sharp, frozen-in-timeless-beauty ravine and gasped from the thrilling ride and the stunning vistas. Even though the chopper is crazy noisy, all you can hear is the serenity outside. Alaska must be what owning and truly loving a dog is like¡ everywhere you look you want to hold it in your mind and caress it and you don't care who sees you because it actually is just you and it alone.

As I landed on a blindingly white glacier, I saw the sled dogs jumping around and even before I de-choppered I heard them yelping as they strained against their chains. They get as excited as Baby's dog Joker used to, pre-skillet, to pull sleds¡ whether it's tourists full of cruise ship buffet food or for the grueling, eleven hundred-mile long Iditarod.

Only if the time is right, I'll like to earn the privilege of sharing my life with a dog. I'd love to feel what my friends feel -- that unconditional, constantly-surprised love when I walk through the door for the one thousandth time.

Dogs' lives are too short. Their only fault, really.

-- Agnes Sligh Turnbull

Head to the Sky

A Story from the National Mill Dog Rescue

Windy spent thirteen years living in a cage, having litter after litter of puppies, fearing humans and suffering with a mammary tumor the size of a hot water bottle, until The National Mill Dog Rescue rescued her in June 2011. The following story was written by the person whose heart she now owns, in her last and forever home.

So, I saw a lot of posts from my friend a number of months back about some group called National Mill Dog Rescue. Being a dog lover, I looked through their page and of course was moved by all the wonderful dogs. Through my life I have had so many loving pups in all different sizes, colors, and breeds. I have adored each one and they each have their own place in my heart.

I was browsing through the available dogs pictures on NMDR's site and my eyes fell upon an itty bitty Iggie named Windy. Her eyes were the eyes of my very beloved rescued ex-racing greyhound that I had lost to cancer. I stared at Windy and then left the page... after all, I have two dogs and I help watch my daughter's dog and cat. Surely there is no more room!

But every day I would go on the site to see if this li'l fourteen-year-old Windy had found her forever home, and each day there she was looking back at me with those sad empty eyes, just as my greyhound had the day we brought him home.

"Okay, okay" I finally said, "I'll adopt this li'l girl." After all, she deserved to have her own family before leaving a world that had been so cruel to her prior to her being rescued by NMDR.

Some people said, "Wow, you really won't have much time to bond with her, she's pretty old and you know you get attached."

I said, "No, it's not like that. This li'l girl is way too damaged in life to bond, I just want her to have a soft bed and a sweet place to live. I will take the best care of her but I don't expect anything back."

She came to us and we named her Olive. She was so timid, she wouldn't come near me. She watched my every move so that she could maneuver away when necessary. She was very sweet, but only felt safe on her new bed.

She favored our old Doxie, but it was what I expected - too "damaged" for real bonding. I would make sure she was cared for.

But then something strange started happening. I would leave the room and look behind me only to see her peeking around the corner. I would turn back, and she would run to her bed. I thought, "That's cute." Then she started coming into the kitchen when I was cooking, keeping her distance but watching with those eyes. It made me smile.

After awhile, she started coming up and into her pack family when it was treat time - she wanted to be near them and strangely, near to me as well. Too damaged? It made me feel so happy for her. Then one day I was sitting on the floor and I reached out to her, like I had a zillion times before, but this time she came to me and licked my hand. My eyes welled up with tears and as I looked at her, she wagged her li'l pretty much hairless tail at me.

I looked into those eyes and she told me "Yes, I am very damaged, but look again because I am in here." Too damaged to bond? NO, not true at all!

One day she ran outside and played with her pack family. Then she stopped, sat down, closed her eyes and raised her head to the sky and just felt the warm sun and light breeze - and at that moment, the door to my heart opened wide and she ran in! I adore her as much as a person can adore anyone. No different if I had gotten her when she was 8 weeks old. She's my precious li'l girl and I think she's beautiful in every way. I love how her tongue hangs out. I love her wrinkled neck. Her once broken tail. Her scars. She's beautiful.

Don't get me wrong - when I go to pick her up, she hides her face and falls down in horror. When I go to get her and the other dogs out of the big kennel she is jumping and barking...   until the door opens and she automatically runs to the back corner and hides her face and shakes. I crawl in and talk to her, then bring her out, and she looks at me as if to say, "Oh! Hi Mommy. I didn't know it was you." But she also loves to snuggle with her brother and sisters, and she falls asleep in my arms now, and puts up with me washing her face and putting a special lotion on her dry skin.

What I have learned is that a dog can forgive, can love again (or for the very first time) when love is given her. When I see her li'l tail wagging at me, I know that I was the one who rescued her. And I've learned to think of things differently. She's not damaged, no. She's perfect.

I think dogs are the most amazing creatures; they give unconditional love. For me they are the role model for being alive.

-- *Gilda Radner*

Casper

by Sharyl Norman

It was as if a camera was panning out from the scene, looking from a corner of the room. A middle-aged woman lay on the bed, her arms wrapped around a black dog that stretched the length of her body and pressed tight against her. A red and white dog was lying next to the bed and a small gray calico cat perched on her hip. All were perfectly still and then slowly, silently the tears began to fall until they turned into sobs. Tears of grief, anger, frustration, and exhaustion all rolling into a small stream winding its way from her cheek to the sleek black fur where she rested her head. A reddish nose inched up the side of the bed and touched her lightly on her back, checking, always checking on her, yet vigilant in his duties as guardian of the door. They were both working dogs, cattle dogs, always needing a job to do.

The Red Heeler's job had been clear from the time he came home ¨C wherever she was, he was. That was his job. He really didn't care to chase cows, he wanted to be close to her. Casper, the black Kelpie, was still in transition. His old job had been to help his owner with work on the ranch and to provide companionship for a man who desperately needed a friend but couldn't bring himself to trust anyone enough to be one. He still had a leather glove that smelled of the man, and the woman let him sleep with it but guarded it carefully from the other dogs. He missed the man and sometimes he got to make the trip to Denver to see him. They both missed the ranch. It had to be sold when the man started undergoing dialysis three times a week. He had tried to keep the dog but apartment life didn't suit either of them well so he had called the woman. Could she keep the dog for just a few weeks until he got better? He knew that one day he could get a house, one with a fence so the dog couldn't go exploring.

However, he had had his claim in with the VA for many years to compensate him for the damage done to his health by his time in Vietnam. There were signals that something might be happening but only his hope and his dream of the house, the fence and his dog kept him going through the process. He had been given the dog by the woman when he was but a puppy and he gave him to his daughter as a gift, but the dog chose him. Their brief visits were high points for both dog and man, and became increasingly difficult for the woman. The man laughed, the dog licked him and leapt into his lap and the woman would smile until they drove away.

Then she would sigh and a few tears would seep from her tightly closed lids. She honored their relationship and each time the man called to say the dog would be coming back to her she was glad for her, sad for him. She tried not to get too attached to the dog, tried to protect her feelings and her heart but he stole them away. He had become the best friend of the Heeler and they explored the pastures and prairie together, chasing rabbits and magpies but never catching either. Sometimes in the midst of the chase they got so excited they ran into each other, knocking them entirely out of the race.

Most days they got along well, the Kelpie knew he could be next to the woman except when they were outside, and then the Heeler was always between them. The woman had been good to the Kelpie. She had found a way to get him to her, using a network of warehouses and truckers to make the journey. She took him with her whenever possible and arranged for his care when she had to be gone for work.

And now, she was hurting. He knew that when the man had been hurting he had been able to help by pressing himself tight against him so he tried that now with her. He knew she had been holding this in for a long time; she felt she had to be strong for all of them, all of the creatures that inhabited her world and that the man who called himself her husband was now gone. It was good riddance, but he and the Heeler knew the danger was not gone, only absent. He had heard the anger in his voice, seen him berate the woman and lunge toward her. He and the Heeler had stayed close as she held her ground, but they knew not to growl out loud because that would intensify the blast of anger.

The Kelpie knew that the only way the woman slept was in small bits and pieces, awakened by each small noise, whether in the house or in her head. There were times when he and the Heeler stood guard all night to let her know that they were there and ready. They stayed near her during the days when she worked outside and they protested going to their kennels when her work called her away.

Her work seemed noxious as well. She came home exhausted and drained from days away. It was on those nights that sleep came hardest. The dreams would wake her and she would read, trying to find some relief in the world outside. It had been that way for months when one day they spent the entire day outside working in the spring sunshine. She curried all of the horses, cleaning away their winter coats and removing the tangles from manes and tails. It was the first day they had all played together for a long time. She laughed and they delighted in the sound, running and jumping just to hear it again.

That night, she felt truly tired and needed to sleep, so the Kelpie and the Heeler took their positions while the cat was not to be left out. She began to relax and then it happened. All of the energy spent holding all of it in was not enough to keep the lids on the boxes of her emotions. The horses, the sunshine, the dogs and the day had let her guard down and now the dam was breaking. The small cracks in her veneer were splitting wide open, letting all of the hurt and anger and grief pour out and onto his black shiny fur.

He breathed in and out, knowing eventually her breath would match his and this tsunami of emotion would be over.

He felt her reach for the cat to scratch her ears. She always had itchy ears. Then for the head of the Heeler which was propped on the bed, letting him know she felt his strength keeping her safe. And then finally...she slept.

Their journey was far from over. There were many days of joy, of grief, of anxiety, of keeping the emotions in and of letting them out. They were all together: the Kelpie, the Heeler, the cat, the horses and the woman. And that was enough. It was enough to rebuild a life that had felt shattered and weak. Rebuild it into a life that was vibrant and strong. With the love of a Kelpie, a Heeler, a cat and the herd of horses who never gave up on the woman who had never given up on them.

"Dogs are not our whole life, but they make our lives whole."

-- Roger Caras

Cowboy Up

by Mark German and Susan Herbert

A beautiful red merle Australian Shepherd was found wandering the streets of Keller, Texas in the summer of 2012. It is unknown how long he was on his own. He was eventually picked up by an Animal Control Officer, brought to Keller Animal Control, and placed on stray hold.

During that summer, Susan Herbert, a graduate of Mark German's *America's Canine Academy*, had been volunteering at that shelter. As she walked down the corridor past the dog kennels, Susan just barely caught a glimpse of him through the corner of her eye. She stopped suddenly and backed up to get a better look.

There was something special about this dog. She quickly noticed that while all of the other dogs were barking and jumping wildly, this dog was just lying there calm, cool, and collected by the gate to his kennel. Not a peep out of him. He looked up at Susan and it was like he was saying, "Hey there, don't mind me, I'm just waitin' for my ride."

At that exact moment, Susan decided that if no one came to claim him, he was coming home with her. There was no way she was going to let him stay there. Five days later, his stray hold was up and no one had come for him. Susan went immediately to rescue him and she chose his name on the way home. She decided to call him "Cowboy".

Having four dogs already, Susan knew she wouldn't be able to keep Cowboy, so her intentions were to adopt him to a good family that would love him and take care of him. Cowboy had some health issues that needed to be addressed first. His skin was a terrible mess and he spent most of the day itching and scratching from dry, scaly and scabby skin. His teeth were a mess also, badly discolored, and he had horribly bad breath. He wouldn't eat dry dog food because it hurt too much to chew it.

After starting his medical treatment, Cowboy settled in with Susan's pack pretty smoothly. He was sweet, loving, and very well behaved. He was not very active, though; he mainly liked to lie down close by Susan. The veterinarian had estimated his age to be about six or seven.

During a trip to Texas, Mark met Cowboy and took a liking to him, mentioning to Susan that he would like to adopt Cowboy, take him back home to Kansas and train him to be his service dog. When Mark was younger, he had served eighteen years as a corpsman in the U.S. Navy and has been diagnosed with post-traumatic stress disorder (PTSD).

A week later, Susan took Cowboy to the veterinarian again, to see what could be done about his teeth. Cowboy was placed under anesthesia and seven teeth were pulled. The veterinarian explained that in order even to reach his teeth, they had had to clear away a lot of hair, grass, and feces. Cowboy was chewing on anything he could find in a desperate attempt to sooth the agonizing pain in his mouth from his rotting teeth and gums!

The next day, Cowboy was like a different dog. No longer sedentary, he got up and began playing with the rest of the pack. He was like a puppy again, happy and energetic and vigorous!

The next month, Mark came for Cowboy. They immediately bonded and were perfect for each other. Cowboy became completely devoted to his pack leader, and he went **everywhere** with Mark. Always patient and friendly with other dogs, Cowboy would assist Mark when evaluating client's dogs, and he never reacted at all if another dog was aggressive toward him. He would simply look up at Mark as if to say, "Dad, I know you are going to handle this, so I'll just wait over here." Cowboy did not need a leash; he was never far away from Mark. Susan can recall several instances when she would see Mark looking around fervently for him saying, "Where's Cowboy? I can't find him."

Amused, Susan would answer, "Turn around Mark, he is right behind you."

After retiring from the military, Mark built a career working with dogs, but none ever had quite the impact on Mark that Cowboy did. Cowboy was able to change Mark, something no other human or animal had been able to do. With Cowboy as his loyal companion, Mark grew softer and happier. Cowboy provided unconditional love and understanding. Cowboy possessed traits that Mark had long been searching for from the people in his life, such as honesty and reliability. Mark would call out, "Cowboy Up!", and every single time, without fail, Cowboy would be there. He could always count on Cowboy, always . . . until the day came.

That day came much sooner than expected. In the end, Mark only had one year with Cowboy. At the end of June, 2013, Cowboy fell ill. He was suddenly no longer able to urinate or eliminate. Susan rushed him to her local veterinarian who found a very progressive prostate tumor the size of a large egg. Susan's vet immediately routed them to an internal medicine DVM for an ultrasound, and after consulting with the oncologist, it was decided that Cowboy would not be coming home. On that day, Cowboy rode west over the rainbow bridge.

Mark and Susan had eventually become business partners and Mark had moved to Texas. In fact, Cowboy had helped to train Susan's service dog, Maverick. Cowboy and Maverick were best friends and traveling buddies. They were all terribly saddened, but especially Mark; he was completely devastated over the loss of his best friend.

Over the next few days the important role that Cowboy played in keeping Mark grounded and in providing emotional support became profoundly clear. The old Mark started coming back; the depression, anger, impatience, and withdrawal.

Everything in life happens exactly as it should, **believe in that** if you can believe in nothing else. There is a reason that Susan walked into the shelter and found Cowboy that day. Someone, somewhere, is always in charge of the master plan. No door is closed, without another being opened.

Two days after Cowboy passed, a good friend in animal rescue called and said she knew that it might be too soon, but they had a litter of seven orphaned Aussie pups whose mother was hit by a car, and she asked if Mark would like a pup. One male pup in particular was a "real toot" and they would love Mark to have him. She said his name is "Buckaroo."

Buck a roo (bə-kə-'rü) *noun*   Definition: Cowboy

Cowboy left his paw prints in the lives of many, not just Mark and Susan. The following are some of the comments written after Cowboy passed on:

-- *I know he is forever thankful for the care and love you provided him with and will forever have a very special place in not only your heart, but of all those lives he touched. What a special dog.*

-- *Such a great dog and he left a HUGE impact on people.*

-- *So sorry for your loss Mark. We'll all miss him. Sad day.*

-- *I am glad to have had the chance to be around him. He was a great dog.*

-- *I am so saddened by the loss of such a great teacher; he was so patient with my dog Redmond.*

-- *We'll miss you Cowboy. You were so special to those that knew you.*

Winchester Remington 5-O

by Julie Poland

I was very excited about our new house. I had been through the end of a marriage, partly the result of ongoing struggles with infertility. I left a 10-year career after an ill-advised relationship that I entered with my eyes wide open, knowing that it would likely mean a major change of venue for me.

The house was a symbol of my collection of fresh starts, of reinventions. Upon leaving my job I opened a corporate and executive coaching practice that I talked about for years prior, and this place was going to be headquarters as well as my residence. It was a baby Victorian, a balloon constructed cottage of 2-1/2 stories that was most recently painted a nauseating combo of banana yellow and mint green. We took it down to the framing with the help of a local contractor and built our new-old house on a street that was an oasis of turn-of-the-century architectural gems.

My new husband, a fellow city dweller who shared my enjoyment of all things aesthetic, helped me search through architectural warehouses for stained-glass windows and an authentic (and incredibly heavy) claw-foot tub. But when all was done, including a lovely flower garden and goldfish pond with fountain, the house was still missing something.

I knew going into this second marriage that children the old-fashioned way might not be an option for me, and I needed something – somebody – to take care of. This house would not be quite a home for me until we had a dog.

My husband grew up with a Corgi, but I always had a soft spot for Cocker Spaniels, and I found an ad for chocolate Cocker puppies within a reasonable drive of our town. We chose a little male who chomped down on my husband's shoelaces, tugged and growled a tiny little growl. And I compromised with my Son-of-an-Air-Force-Master-Sergeant by giving MY dog Chester the official moniker Winchester Remington 5-0.

Our little gem of a neighborhood was surrounded by sidewalks and little grass. In addition, the next streets in all directions were litter-filled and occupied at every hour of the day and night by people hustling drugs or more personal services. It became our habit to walk Chester, our little brown Cocker Spaniel, around the block, and we would chuckle to ourselves when the more unsavory characters would jump out of the way onto the stoops and into the breezeways to avoid Chester's oh-so-lethal little teeth.

My husband told the little kids nearby that Chester was able to sniff drugs, and we could see the message spread down the street and around the corner as we stood talking to the elderly neighbors in the big green Victorian. Surreptitious glances in our direction preceded casual strolls to the next block over. Our little 5-0 helped us develop and maintain a zone of safety around our neighborhood.

We went a little bit overboard with him, revealing to witnesses that he was a child substitute for us. I bought him color-coordinated harnesses and leashes, and even found a denim Harley Davidson vest for him to wear. It wasn't really to keep him warm, even though I claimed that the Cocker cut was a bit chilly across the back in the midst of winter weather. I thought it was cute. And I was thoroughly ridiculed by some of my friends who thought that no self-respecting dog should be caught wearing it.

We took Chester for walks on the grounds of a nearby park, where at the age of two he got too curious around a bee and was stung on the eye. His eye swelled way up, and didn't improve after the vet gave us some medicine for him. Ultimately we received a referral to a veterinary eye specialist, where we found out that he had severe glaucoma, a condition to which Cocker Spaniels can be predisposed.

Despite surgery to relieve the pressures in his eyes and daily meds that stretched our startup business owners' budget, Chester lost most of his vision.

After five years we adopted our first child, and Chester guarded her crib. By now he was feeling his way by patting his front paws cautiously in front of him as he moved forward, but he was quick to alert us if our baby daughter started to cry. He walked beside her stroller at the local college, a place less likely than the park to present unpredictable obstacles for him, with a nice flat pathway and plenty of trees that needed watering. Our baby daughter said his name "Det-doe" before she said "mama".

Despite his infirmity Chester lived until after our daughter's 4th birthday. We knew he was becoming more and more tentative when he picked his way down the wooden staircase from the second floor to the first. Then one morning he was unable to support his weight on his back legs. We knew it was time for us to let him go.

My husband had a cast made of his webbed paw, big for such a small dog. We wept and wept the first couple of days, especially when we overheard our preschooler daughter reciting a little ditty she created about her now-dead dog. He was our first child and our daughter's first friend. He made our first house a home, and helped us prepare to be parents. The feeling he created in our house made us certain that we would always make sure we had a dog in our house. But he was the first. Chester was a good dog.

Chester sending our eldest, Lauren, off to her first day of pre-school

Taylor Bay: Potcake from Paradise - A Tale of Love, Loss, and Renewal

by Anthony Bennie

The story of Taylor Bay began on the island of Providenciales, in the Turks and Caicos Islands. She and her five Potcake littermates were tiny two-week-old pups with little chance of survival when they were pulled from the scrubby grass off the beach, but they were among the lucky ones rescued by the Potcake Foundation and TCSPCA. They received vet care, and were housed and fed with a chance to be adopted.

Potcakes are the indigenous mixed breed dogs of the Turks and Bahamas islands. Dogs were traditionally fed the hard chunks of residual rice, peas, fat, and meat from the bottom of a stew pot that's been cooked over open flame. These hard chunks are called potcakes, and the dogs became known as Potcakes by association with their food.

Over the past few hundred years, a "stew" of dogs from many breeds brought by voyagers from all over the world have been tossed into the island melting pot to become today's Potcakes. Though they can vary quite a bit in size and color, there's a "Potcake look" that one comes to recognize after spending time in the Islands. They are recognized as a distinct breed by the Royal Bahamian kennel club, but still are considered "mixed breed" in the U.S. Despite a long career in pet care and nutrition, I had never heard of a Potcake dog.

This story, however, is not just about adopting a strange dog in a strange land; it's about the spiritual cycle of love, loss, and renewal that is inherent in the love of dogs. The unlikely twists and cosmic convergences that led to our becoming "Potcake parents" may suggest to some that there are spirit hands, or perhaps a billion invisible paws, helping to drive the life cycle forward.

Taylor Bay's trip from the tropical sun of Turks and Caicos to a Connecticut snowstorm really started as a conversation with Isis, our then seven year old Golden Retriever. By "conversation," I don't mean the usual chatter that we humans inflict on our dogs as an antidote to our own loneliness and boredom; I mean a genuine conversation, in which Isis transmitted thoughts and images to me with a clarity and intensity that was startling, even disturbing.

After finishing work late one night in January of 2011, I tiptoed into the bedroom, hoping to wake neither my wife, nor Isis and our other Golden, four year old Ozzy. But while getting ready for bed, I felt an urgent mental tug from Isis that compelled me to lie down next to her.

A rush of thoughts and images came to me from Isis. Of course it sounds insane, but the things coming into my head didn't sound like my own thoughts, and the message was clear: Isis was afraid of dying. I saw images of our departed dogs, Carly and Charlie. Isis had lived with both of them as they grew old, with everything that entailed, including their eventually leaving us. She wanted NOTHING to do with the aging process and its embarrassing loss of mobility and control. And she was worried about all of us, especially her mate Ozzy. She didn't want to let us all down by dying.

This was craziness. Isis was a healthy seven year old with many great years ahead of her, right? So I tried to send out waves of formed thoughts and images, like pictures within clouds, pictures of happy things like swimming, chasing balls, romping with Ozzy and the kids; things I felt sure she had so much more of too experience.

Shortly after our late night conversation, Isis started making an occasional scratchy sound in her throat, and after a few days of this we took her to the vet. We found out that she had advanced cancer, which had spread to her lungs, and that there was little we could do for her. On one of her last nights, she rallied and played with Ozzy like old times, and I was optimistic. Two days later, Isis died in our arms while we lay with her on blankets covering the floor of the vet office.

Amanda and I sank deeply into grief. Watching Isis die so quickly when we had no idea she was even sick was a sharp sword to our hearts. And I couldn't really grasp the truth that she had TOLD me she was dying.

Months earlier, we had planned a first ever family vacation to Turks and Caicos, in part to celebrate my parents upcoming 60th Anniversary. That trip was now two weeks away, and we almost canceled, but it would have been selfish to do this to our children and parents. Isis would want us to go, we told each other.

So as our family flew towards the Caribbean, I thumbed through the official Turks and Caicos tourist magazine publication in the seat pocket. My "dogdar" led me to an article about Potcakes and the Potcake rescue foundation. It was weighing on us that Ozzy was grieving as well, and that after being with Isis his whole life, he needed company and would not thrive as a solo dog. We touched down in Providenciales, known as Provo by both locals and tourists. Potcakes were forgotten as we landed and dove into exploring. We would wait until we returned home to methodically search for a new companion for Ozzy, to keep the cycle turning.

However, the universe works in strange ways. The first time we drove down the remote beach road looking for our rental house, located between Sapodilla Bay and Taylor Bay, just three houses down from our destination we passed a house with a wrought iron gate sculpted as a dog's profile. Again, my "dogdar" perked up, and doubly so , when I saw that the house had a name- "Maison de Chiens." Even with my rudimentary high school French, I knew this meant "house of the dogs"! What were the odds that my wife and I, both pet nutrition business veterans, would randomly rent a house online, and wind up so close to a fellow dog fanatic?

But even after that nudge, we had no more thoughts of banging on the gates of Maison de Chiens, or of looking more deeply into the Potcake situation.

Or so we thought. On a visit to a restaurant near the rental house, we happened to meet a wonderful man named Lovey Forbes, who turned out to be one of the most well-known and best loved musicians in the islands. As a musician myself, I was thrilled to meet him. After we had discussed the music, Lovey asked us the fateful question: "What do YOU do?"

"We own a company called Clear Conscience Pet and we manufacturer healthy dog treats," I answered. This reply prompted a huge smile from Lovey. "You're kidding, Mon, my wife is the head of the Potcake Foundation." My jaw dropped. When we asked Lovey where he lived, we hardly needed to listen to the answer. Of course, it was Maison de Chiens! Lovey's wife, artist Heather Simpson-Forbes, was the Founder and Chairwoman of the Potcake Foundation, the only charitable organization dedicated exclusively to bettering the life and health of Potcake dogs in the Turks and Caicos islands.

Now if one is looking for signs of that invisible force at work, this was a persuasive example. What were the odds that of all places in the world, we would wind up in front of this man, at this moment, on this island thousands of miles from home? How could this all be chalked up to "coincidence"?

We were graciously invited to Heather and Lovey's bayfront villa that evening, where we met our first four Potcakes dogs, the current pack in the Forbes home. They were friendly and fun. Potcakes were pretty cool!

By the end of the night, we were set up to meet Susan Blehr, the Director of the Turks and Caicos SPCA (TCSPCA). Our goal was still only to visit the facility, to make a donation of money and treats to support the rescue efforts. We most CERTAINLY were not going to look at puppies to adopt!

We and our two boys made the trip to the TCSPCA office and met Susan. After some general discussion, she said, "now aren't you really here to look at puppies? We have some who are ready for new homes right now." My hands got clammy and Amanda and I looked at each other. "Uh, well, we really couldn't possibly bring home a new puppy," I said. We explained about our recent loss of Isis, our concerns about introducing a semi-wild dog to our family, and of course worries that Ozzy would reject a strange new dog so soon after losing his lifetime mate.

We also had concerns about the long term health of Potcakes, about whom we had known nothing only days before. And what about the practical considerations of traveling for hours on an airplane and going through customs with a non-housebroken puppy? Impossible!

Susan reassured us on all fronts. The TCSPCA has placed thousands of puppies in homes in the U.S.A. and Canada, and has the process down to a science, she told us. Health certificates are supplied for travel, all puppies ready for adoption have had complete veterinary care including all required shots, and the puppy would be given to us in a pet carrier at the airport on our departure day with all papers. We would only need to take the puppy's paperwork to the airline counter and pay a $100 fee to take the puppy in the plane for the trip home.

Reluctantly, we followed Susan from the TCSPCA office to the Pampered Paws kennel, knowing that leaving the office and going to the kennel was a huge step. The kennel was very clean and well-run, and the dogs were in large runs with plenty of running room rather than confined to kennel cages.

It was here that we first saw three puppies, two females and a male that had been rescued in late November at less than two weeks old as part of a litter of six from an area near the beach. Their survival had been doubtful, but the pups received excellent veterinary care, and they pulled through. By the time we visited, three had been adopted and the remaining three were about twelve weeks old. They needed homes very soon or they would get too big to fit in a hand held carrier for the flight back to the USA. Without off-island adoption, their future was uncertain. So this was the moment of truth. Would we form a bond with a Potcake puppy and cast aside our fears?

One of the females was very shy and frightened, but she went to my older son and nuzzled him. The others were more playful, but when this little girl looked right at me with her beautiful brown eyes, I knew I was in trouble. We were told that this puppy might not be our best choice, as she was very fearful and might have a harder time adapting. But I saw something in those eyes that anyone who has ever rescued a dog will understand; it was a plea for life and an offer of unconditional lifetime love. And maybe something else¡ a twinkle that felt like Isis saying "yes, she's the one"! My heart melted along with my resistance, and we made a family decision to take a leap of faith and rescue this little girl, making her a part of our family.

The next day, Susan brought the puppy to the airport to meet us. We decided to call our new baby "Taylor Bay," after the location where we rented our island house. She behaved beautifully during the flight, making barely a peep. Her first experience in Connecticut was stepping out of the car and into over two feet of snow! Not exactly Caribbean weather, but she surprised us by being more curious than concerned!

Ozzy, our Golden boy, was a little shocked at first that we had brought this strange looking creature home with us and was no doubt still in mourning for his mate. But after a few days, he warmed up to her. Since then they have become inseparable. Her shyness melted away with the snow by spring, and she has become a vibrant and loving 40 pound adult. Her personality is cautious with anyone new, and she's an alert watchdog, but she loves people and warms up to strangers quickly once she feels safe. Few can resist her unusual "dingo-like" appearance and her winning personality.

We hope our story can give some comfort and hope to those wounded by the grief of losing a beloved dog. No dog "replaces" another, of course. You'll grieve as hard as you must, and you'll cry as many tears as you think you can produce and still find more. But keep your heart open. Somewhere, out there, whether on a faraway island or in a shelter a mile from home, is THE dog that is supposed to come next in your own cycle of life. And who knows? Maybe, just maybe, the dog you think you lost forever is right there in the spirit world, helping you to find the next doggy love in your life.

The greatest healing therapy is friendship and love.

- Hubert Humphrey

"One reason a dog can be such a comfort when you're feeling blue is that he doesn't try to find out why."

-- Author Unknown

Baby Steps

A Story from the National Mill Dog Rescue

We often take things for granted. When you adopt a former mill dog, you suddenly find yourself quietly cheering on the most miniscule things. Like taking a treat from your hand, a wagging tail, playing with a toy.

I have been part of the rescue, rehabilitation and rehoming of many dogs over the years, starting with Min Pins and now Italian Greyhounds. The dogs in my care were not "mine". They were making a short stop on their journey, taking a bit of time to get their bearings and learn proper manners such as potty training, socialization, and leash training. We would go out and meet new people, explore the world and then...when all the stars were in alignment, the right family would come along and they were on their way again, towards a new life.

A few months ago, I was screening homes for an Italian Greyhound who was being fostered locally by a friend. I had a few homes lined up when I received the e-mail that I knew deep down was coming. She couldn't part with him and had applied to adopt him. About the same time, I heard that National Mill Dog Rescue had 9 Italian Greyhounds waiting to be adopted, so I contacted Theresa Strader to see if she would consider working together. There was a voicemail waiting for me when I arrived at home. Not only would they consider it, they were over the moon!

I learned more about each of the Iggies and went about trying to find them homes. Then something happened that I rarely experience: I fell for one of the fosters. I called Theresa's husband, Rich to chat about Cricket and found out that she wasn't going to work for me. So I pulled the website up on my laptop while I still had him on the phone and perused the rest of the photos. I asked about Viper, but again not a good fit. I took a deep breath and uttered the words that would change my life forever.

"Well, do you have anyone there that you're especially worried about?"

That's when Rich told me about Izzy. She'd been at the kennel for 2 years. They tried placing her in a foster home twice but it just didn't work. Rich was very fond of her and also very worried that she would never find a home of her own. Always up for a challenge, I agreed to take her and said that if for some reason she didn't work out, I would work night and day to find her a new home.

I know a couple who have a Chihuahua who was rescued from a puppy mill. I was at their home one night and they were raving about her "Thundershirt", which is a wrap that works by applying constant, gentle pressure to the torso, helping to combat a dog's anxiety, fear, stress, and over-excitement. I had heard of them but never used one before. I asked about it and they gave me a little demonstration. While using it was as if she was a different dog! I mentioned this to Rich while we were busy arranging transport for Izzy and three other dogs from NMDR up here to Alberta, Canada. He said they had a few but he hadn't tried them out yet. So he sent one up with Izzy. It took over a week before I got up the courage to put it on her but once I did, she was more relaxed. I call it her "Magic Shirt"!

To say that Izzy was timid, however, would be a gross understatement. Unfortunately, this is common for Italian Greyhounds who spend most of their lives in wire cages at puppy mills, deprived of human contact. She accepted dogs. It was me she wasn't willing to trust and wanted nothing to do with. For three days I thought she was deaf until I uttered the magic word - "TREAT". For the most part, I couldn't get near her. If I walked by the dog bed she'd claimed as her own, she would get up and run away. If I looked at her too long... spoke to her... aimed the camera at her, she would run away. I had to corral her to pick her up and she would stiffen in my arms, pushing away with all four legs and leaning her head backwards to avoid being anywhere near me. On top of that, she would pee on me! But because I knew all too well where she had come from, the life she had before NMDR stepped in and helped her, I was willing to let her come around on her own time.

Time went on and I noticed not only her demeanor but her behavior changing. She started allowing me to pick her up. She no longer scurried around and startled every time I moved. She no longer ran away if I looked at her, spoke to her, took her picture or walked by her bed in the living room.

Now, if I go into another room, she will sometimes follow me. This little dog, (who for the first few weeks at my home did not move from the dog bed) will follow me down the hallway and come into my bedroom. I have learned not to pay too much attention to her, to allow her to just mill about. Otherwise, she's off again, heading for her little bed where she feels secure and comfortable. She no longer needs to be carried up and down the stairs, provided you turn the light on(she has cataracts). She no longer runs for cover if I opened the fridge. She no longer pees on me when I pick her up.

About a week ago, Izzy started doing something that touched my heart: she wagged her tail! This little Iggie, who scurried around the house with her tail tucked between her legs, looked at me and...it wasn't a random occurrence. She was wagging her tail at me! Not wanting to freak her out, I kept my joy hidden from her and acted as though it was completely normal. The good news is that her tail wags all the time now and it's a beautiful sight!

Since then she's attempted to play with toys – twice! As with all mill dogs, she's not all that sure what they're for or how this whole "playing" thing works but I've watched her watching the other dogs and am so pleased that she's even the slightest bit interested.

I have a dog room downstairs with an ex-pen where the dogs stay when I am not at home and at night. When I get home after work, I go downstairs and let them out of their pen. They go into their crates and have their supper When she arrived, I would have to corral her and then put her in the crate to eat. Then she decided she would get in there all by herself, thank you very much. Right about the time her tail started wagging, she decided that it would be fun to play with the Brand New Momma. She dances around, watching me make each of the meals and putting them in the crates. Then it's her turn. She waits for me to put the bowl in the crate, then her head darts in and out. Then she does a little dance. This continues for a bit, until she decides to go in on her own or I am able to guide her in.

I took her "Magic Shirt" off last night to wash it and noticed that she's gained some muscle tone. I take it off her every few days to brush her coat and check to ensure her skin isn't rubbing or otherwise causing her discomfort. So far, so good. It was still wet this morning, so I left it off her for the day and we'll see how she feels when I get home tonight. If this one should wear out, I am more than willing to buy her another... and another... and another after that. It is my hope that one day she will no longer need it but it's totally up to her. I am fully prepared for the fact that she may decide – like Linus with his blanket – she needs it to feel OK about the world.

Baby steps. It's all about the baby steps.

"His ears were often the first thing to catch my tears."

Elizabeth Barrett Browning

A Healing Bond

by Cheryl Arnold Moseley

His name was Bond.

But not the infamous one; rather, he was a 99-lb secret agent of a different sort—my German shepherd.

He, too, was professionally trained, and was also fearless ,confident, intelligent, and loyal. Yet, he was a true savings bond; he saved my life and soul in a way that no human could.

Bond's impact was immediate; his name epitomized the everlasting legacy he left behind.

It's virtually impossible to tell Bond's story without telling parts of my own.

I was born and raised in Venice, California. My mother was a courageous and resilient woman; my father, despite being born totally blind, was a chiropractor. He was a man so multi-faceted, and so blessed with a razor-sharp sense of humor, that he conveyed wisdom and inspiration to everyone. His cherished seeing eye dog, Rex, a large German shepherd we adored and trusted, fit seamlessly into our lives during my young childhood. Our home was full of fun, joy, music, and great times.

As idyllic as all of this might sound, I did not live in a Norman Rockwell painting. There was a world out there full of wars, violence, and man's inhumanity to man. When I became a nurse I became increasingly aware of violence, as I treated stabbing and shooting victims in the hospital.. I even managed to avoid a few dangerous encounters while walking to and from my car, as well as being robbed.

My work and my avocations of photography and outdoor adventure took me all over the world. And it was on one of my journeys that violence struck me directly: I was raped, brutally beaten, and left for dead. By some miracle, I managed to survive and recover; but the indelible scars to my psyche and soul felt almost insurmountable. I did not know if I would ever feel safe again.

Having experienced the joy and comfort of Rex, it made sense to me to try to find a great dog—one just like him. A dog like this could help me heal, I knew, especially because memories of my father and his beloved Rex were virtually intertwined. With all the work and traveling, however, I had not yet acquired a home large enough to house a dog. It wasn't until I married the man of my dreams, a neurosurgeon with whom I had worked for over a decade, that we could finally have a home fit to properly accommodate a dog.

As my husband and I set out to design and build a home in Montana, crime struck our lives again. Just before we moved in, someone broke in and stole thousands of dollars' worth of saws, drills, subcontractors' equipment, and uninstalled plumbing fixtures—even sinks and toilets. I was irate! True, no one died. No one was hurt, since we weren't there when it happened.

But the nightmares of being raped and robbed returned.

It was time to find the German shepherd that I had been dreaming about since I was a child—a dog like Rex. My husband had recently insisted that my mother move to Montana to live with us. She had also been robbed in her home, and had been a victim of two other large crimes. As we were unpacking, I said to my husband, "The time has come. I don't want just any pet. I want a German Shepherd that is a professionally trained protection dog.

By this time in life, my father had died. I missed him but was happy to have my sweet and spunky mother living with us. As we unpacked together, we each found our caches of photos, string-wrapped stacks of letters, journals, and a purple orchid corsage to the prom. We finally had a home for our life's treasure, room for all the books belonging to our parents and grandparents back to 1850s. I had never before had a place to put the things that mattered.

Out of all the memorabilia, including my father's volumes of a Braille Bible, my greatest treasure was the faded brown leather harness that had belonged to his beloved Rex. I hung his harness on the wall next to the antique bookcase, nearly touching the photo of the two of them from 1940s. On the floor, directly under the hanging harness, I placed Daddy's black leather doctor's bag that he used for house calls, unused for a decade since he died in my arms. It was when he died that I became the protector of the harness that first gave him freedom at seventeen – when the prize he won in a journalism contest was a Seeing Eye dog.

Both my father and Rex seemed to come alive in our home, which gave me such a sense of warmth and security. My husband, my mom, and I talked about them frequently. My mother reminisced about the times when my father used to tell Rex to protect me when he wasn't working as Daddy's eyes. Every Sunday, while he was washing and waxing his pampered 1940's Buick, Mom recalled leaving me in the driveway with them in a wooden baby tenda on wheels. I was with my Daddy all the time--which meant that Rex was right there too.

I loved finally being in our new home in Montana! I found it comforting to be surrounded by memories – old books and photos in every room, even my husband's first football and his stuffed teddy bear without eyes, which I put into a shadow box as a surprise. It was time to look for a dog to be part of our family

I prayed! OK! I'll say it! I wanted bold, beautiful, confident, courageous, strong, sweet, gentle, intelligent, loyal, loving, disciplined, fierce and fearless, but with a calm demeanor. Just like my man! I could see Bond in my mind. It took several months of searching. I traveled across the country to meet him on the east coast, where he had arrived from Czechoslovakia, and I immediately knew he was the one.

After watching his training and personality, I was sure Bond would be a perfect fit for all of us. After having him trained, the trainer brought him to us, where passed his final exam by demonstrating his ability to protect us and defend his new home and his new family.

The first time Bond walked into his new home was overwhelming for me. I opened the garage door for him to enter his new world - one interpreted and predominated by smell. My husband and I lagged behind him; still close enough, however, to watch him as he surveyed his new home, room to room. He sniffed and sniffed, stopping in some places longer than others; assessing a horse blanket from Bhutan, a buffalo skin, hand woven carpets from Azerbaijan and Turkey, a fur hat from the Iditarod dog race, moose and sealskin mukluks that I tanned and sewed 35 years before, along with Eskimo women elders. There were many other precious things, and Bond seemed to give them their due, but in an almost unattached way. It wasn't until he reached my father's doctor bag that Bond's demeanor changed.

He lingered with it. Then, he stretched his nose up high along the wall.

What was he sniffing? Rex's harness had not been used since he died over 40 years ago. Bond sniffed my father's bag again, then, stretched up to the harness for another long whiff.

By this point, Bond had no interest in scouting out the rest of the house. Deliberately, he lay down and curled up with his nose next to the bag, directly under the harness.

Until … another deep breath—as if to confirm what had now become obvious. Bond had found his rightful place; it was right beside my father and Rex. It felt like he had returned home—home to HIS family. Home now, with my family. Home now, with my family.

My face was wet with tears.

My soul found a long sought-after peace. As Bond rested next to my father and Rex, a piece of me could now rest too.

A world restored; the circle was now complete. Bond had "bonded" with all that was right inside me.

Finally.

In the aftermath, as my mind rose to this recognition, I began to wonder many things …

What images did he see with his nose?

How powerful are our thoughts? How much of our own world do we create? Are there past lives? Do angels exist?

Life is a series of tiny miracles.

Bond lived to be 13 years old. He was completely devoted to my mother, John, and me. The following quote must also be true for our beloved dogs and Guardian angels:

"The things which the child loves remain in the domain of the heart until old age. The most beautiful thing in life is that our souls remain hovering over the places where we once enjoyed ourselves, regardless of distance or time."

Khalil Gibran (1883 – 1931)

Bond, my 99-lb secret agent German shepherd.

Because of Liesel

by Jane Procacci

I've always considered myself very fortunate to have grown up around a wide variety of dogs. My parents built and operated a boarding kennel throughout my childhood. We also raised and showed dogs and horses. During the holidays, we easily had over 100 dogs and cats at the kennel. Because of this, I was exposed to many different breeds and sizes of dogs.

I began showing dogs at the age of six and in my later teen years, I went on to begin my apprenticeship as a Professional Handler. Through the years I came in contact with some very special dogs that I shared a unique bond with. You know, the kind of special friend that you just click with? I truly believe those special canine friends got me through my younger years. I could share my deepest, darkest secrets with them and knew that those secrets were safe. These special furry friends helped to mold me in to the person I am today. They taught me about a level of loyalty that no person could ever teach another.

In November of 1997, in my late 30's, I was diagnosed with what was then a rare incurable bladder disease that attacks the auto immune system. In less than a year, I was disabled. I feared my life was over.

We had recently been given a German Shepherd who had been retired from the show ring. She was an exceptional dog with more common sense than many people I knew. She quickly began alerting me as to when my auto immune system was about to crash. I was floored at her natural ability to do this.

She taught me a lot about having a therapy dog and I believe it was in preparation for the amazing furkid that we now have.

Liesel is a 3 legged (tri-paw) mixed breed that we adopted from Monroe, Louisiana in 2011. At 5 months of age, Liesel was found on the side of the road in Monroe with her right rear foot missing. Luckily, a wonderful rescue group in Monroe, Paws Nela, found out about her being at the local shelter and they took her to their vet.

Once Liesel recovered from her amputation surgery she was flown to us in N.C. by volunteer pilots with Pilots N Paws.

Our lives have never been the same! Liesel truly has a gift... she is able to bring a smile to the face of everyone in a room. If you even attempt to ignore her, she'll quickly get one of her toys and put it in your lap. If that doesn't work she'll begin to tap you with her front paw.

Even in the nursing homes that we've taken her to, total strangers open up about a special dog that they had previously had in their life and how much that dog meant to them, all while they were stroking Liesel's soft fur and looking deep into her golden brown eyes.

Just this week, while out in the yard with Liesel, one of our neighbors came outside to tell her husband something. Liesel began whining loudly while looking at this person but the neighbor ignored Liesel. So Liesel begins barking. . .LOUDLY, as if to say "HEY! SPEAK TO ME, HUMAN!!" I began laughing because I knew exactly what Liesel was doing.

Finally, our neighbor said hello to Liesel and Liesel then turned around and walked away.

Liesel also inspires me every day. I look at her and all she went through and realize that she never lets a missing leg stop her from achieving whatever it is that she wants to do or where ever it is that she wants to get. At 35 pounds, she has the heart of a lion. Nothing scares her.

So, when I begin doubting myself, or my capacity to deal with my disability, I stop and think, "Because of Liesel, I can. I can do this"!

Liesel

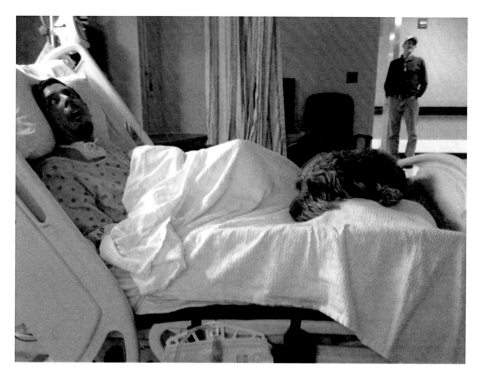

"Dogs don't know about beginnings, and they don't speculate on matters that occurred before their time. Dogs also don't know—or at least don't accept—the concept of death. With no concept of beginnings or endings dogs probably don't know that for people having a dog as a life companion provides a streak of light between two eternities of darkness."

Stanley Coren

Melissa

by Paul Owens

There were 10 students in class, all considered "at-risk." Some were diagnosed with attention deficit disorder and on medication, most lived in poverty, in dangerous neighborhoods, and a few, like Melissa, lived with an aunt or grandmother rather than parents.

Melissa was in the 4th grade. When she first walked into class, I was struck by how drawn and colorless her face was. She walked with a kind of vacant stare, always looking out of the corner of her dark eyes and never looking you in the face. She didn't smile. If you approached her or reached out to touch her arm, she would quickly withdraw and back away. The teachers hoped our animal-assisted therapy program, Paws for Peace, might allow her to reach out to the world a little more.

The first day of class was held without dogs, except for my Portuguese water dog, Molly. Molly has been my trustworthy partner for 8 years and has probably been petted by 5000 children. She helps a child learn how to approach and pet a dog and demonstrates "dog-speak," the body language dogs use to communicate. Molly is God's gift to children, the world, and especially me.

On the second day of class, the children were introduced to their dogs, all primarily rescued dogs from the Glendale Humane Society in California. Melissa's dog was another rescue who recently was adopted by a couple who thought she might benefit from our program. The dog was a five-month-old Whippet named Devo.

At first Melissa didn't know what to make of the jumping, barking little dog but with a lot of gentle encouragement, she hesitantly reached out and began to pet him. Just like the training process with dogs, we let Melissa proceed at her own comfortable speed and by the end of the next day Melissa was sitting on the ground allowing Devo to jump onto her lap and off again. The tightness in her face began to soften and I noticed the faintest glimmer of a smile.

All through week two, most of the children in class progressed rapidly. Two decided they weren't really interested in the responsibilities of feeding and cleaning up the poop and by week three, they were gone. But Melissa never missed a class. The children had the dogs sitting and lying down, staying in place and going to their beds.

They learned they could get their dogs to do all of these things without having to hit, kick, shock, shake, or jerk them on a leash. They trained and groomed their dogs with kindness and affection. They listened to their dog's heartbeat through a stethoscope when a guest veterinarian visited to talk about health and give each dog a vaccination.

The high point of each class however was the daily walk. The children were taught how to hold the leash, how to have their dog sit before crossing the street (it was a low traffic cul-de-sac), and while walking, occasionally ask their dog to come when called. But children being children and dogs being dogs, every walk inevitably turned into a run. Seeing ears flapping, tails wagging and children joyously yelling while running down the hill after their dogs summed up the Paws for Peace program perfectly.

For some of these children, Paws for Peace provides a very rare opportunity for them to just be children. They can have fun in a safe environment. They know they are protected. We see the joy in their beaming faces and feel their happiness and trust.

At the end of the third week, Melissa's mother showed up for class. Parents, guardians, and teachers are always invited to watch the classes. But Melissa lived with her aunt and grandmother.

While I was instructing another student, the mother walked straight up to Melissa, who was seated on the ground with Devo. I couldn't hear what she said but the mother abruptly turned and left and Melissa started to cry. My assistant instructor, Stacy, put her arms around the sobbing little girl and held her. Stacy gave me a sign and the two of them left class for a walk. A few minutes later they returned and Melissa went back to petting little Devo. Stacy signaled that everything was OK and class continued.

After class, I made a point to praise Melissa for her courage and bravery, and she allowed me to give her a little hug. When the children had all left, Stacy related what had happened. Melissa's mother never said hello or acknowledged her. And who knows how long it had been since they had seen each other. She had walked up to this sweet little girl and said, " I think your dog is ugly." Then she left.

Poor little Melissa was heartbroken. I asked Stacy what she had said to console her. She said, "I didn't really know what to say. So I asked her if she thought Devo was beautiful. She nodded her head yes. Then I asked her if she loved Devo. She managed to whisper a yes. So I said it really doesn't matter what other people think sometimes.

All that's important is that you think Devo is beautiful and that you love him....and Devo loves you."

My heart was in my throat and I smiled and thanked Stacy profusely. She was perfect.

From that day on, Melissa began to smile more and she volunteered to clean up after class and to walk the dogs to the cars. At graduation, this shy, wonderful little girl got up in front of forty people and showed them what she had learned in class. Devo sat, laid down, came when called and stayed in position as Melissa walked around him. She knelt down to pet him and give him a treat. And the smile never left her face. For a moment there was silence and then everyone applauded and cheered. We instructors all had tears in our eyes.

It is for children like Melissa the Paws for Peace program was created. One-by-one, with the help of animals, each child learns that there are other ways to get along with family, friends, and the environment -- ways that can replace fear, anger, and frustration.

With the generous assistance of loving volunteers, children learn the value of practicing empathy, respect, nonviolence and responsibility. In short, they learn that kindness and compassion work.

The Home for Wayward Dogs

by LinnieSarah Helpern

In a fairly normal town on a fairly normal street in a fairly normal house, there live five not-so-normal dogs. Walk by this house at any time of day, and a chorus of happy howls and goofy barks of varying degrees will greet you. The five four-legged creatures that roam this home come in all shapes and sizes, from a tiny little rugrat to a giant horse-sized furbaby; yet, they are as much a family as if they had come from the same litter. Each resident of The Home for Wayward Dogs has joined the menagerie by different means: some were homeless, some were sprung from dog jail, and one was even a member of a horrible doggie Fight Club. But each of these sweet angels now have one thing in common: the love of their humans.

The Home for Wayward Dogs began a long time ago in a very different normal house. The original wayward dog, a scruffy mutt with no home of her own, showed up at the human's front door every day with the persistence and adoration that only a pup can muster. A bowl of kibble and some head scratches later, and the Home was born. The pup came first, and a tiny human came later, raised like sisters in The Home for Wayward Dogs. The tiny human learned to walk by holding on to the first dog's tail, and learned also that the best kind of mischief is mischief committed with the aid of a furry friend.

Since that first day, a collection of furbabies has walked in and out of their humans' home, but never out of their hearts. Some have lived in The Home for Wayward Dogs for many years, digging holes and chasing butterflies from puppydom until their sweet noses turned white. Others bounced joyfully through the slobber-coated front door, only to leave unexpectedly, much too soon, taking their gentle spirits and a piece of their humans' hearts with them. It's never easy when a furbaby leaves The Home for Wayward Dogs, but that is the true challenge of being a human there: knowing you will always one day, be left behind.

The five frantic, shedding, hungry, noisy, balls of energy that run around and currently tear apart every inch of The Home for Wayward Dogs can sometimes be exhausting. Sometimes the barking can shake your very core. Sometimes the humans may think the dogs are eating better than they are! They may even be quite confident that these chaotic creatures are the real masters of the house. But all it takes is one gentle nuzzle, one little lick, one silly grin, and the humans remember how each of these pups ended up at The Home to begin with.

Two legs or four legs, everyone deserves to be loved.

"Look deep into the eyes of any animal and then for a moment, trade places, their life becomes as precious as yours and you become as vulnerable as them."

- Philip Ochoa

Barley: Mickey's Son

by Holly Altman

My fiancé says that he knows his place in the pack. It's a partial joke because many times the dog trumps Bob when it comes to receiving my unabashed love and attention. But the truth is that we wouldn't be a pack if it weren't for Barley. I'd never have learned enough about love, flexibility, connection and compromise.

I'll never forget the day I went to pick up my boy in Peoria, Arizona. He was a lanky seven-month-old beauty; a fluffy, blonde goofball. I had lived alone for years, and spent many months debating whether or not to get a dog. I read books, researched, and played out every possible scenario in my head. I met older rescue Golden Retrievers, talked to dog owners, and visited four or five different breeders and their litters. I met Barley's dog family for the first time when he was only a few months old. I didn't meet him exactly, but I met his sister, brother, mother, grandmother, aunts and uncles. He must have been sleeping. His family felt comfortable to me, and made me laugh.

Meeting Barley's family threw me into turmoil. I had bonded with my friend Linda's Golden Retriever, Pacha Mama, during the most difficult emotional transition of my life, and Mama was my soul mate, my earth mother, instilling deep within me a life-changing love for the breed. Mama helped me heal. After Mama moved away having a dog of my own became a relentless longing. But the puppies were only two months old and ready for homes. I didn't know how I would handle a puppy since I lived alone. At the time I worked more than thirty minutes from home, and I certainly couldn't be there to let the puppy out every two hours.

I had never had a dog of my own so I had no confidence in the matter. When I was a kid, our family dog, Sudsy, was a fat, furry white mutt with black spots underneath who roamed the neighborhood. All the dogs ran free in our suburban town of Wayland, Massachusetts in the late 1960's and early 1970's. It was a common occurrence for a neighbor's dog to show up at our doorstep any time, day or night, looking for treats or an adventure. Sudsy frequently took herself to the Villa, the local Italian restaurant, to eat leftovers from the dumpster.

We lived on Barney Hill Road, a quiet, thickly wooded, horseshoe shaped block. Sudsy had a habit of laying down, parked in the middle of the street in front of our house, refusing to move from her perch in the sun. Cars would honk and honk. We were helpless to move Sudsy against her will. Eventually the cars would turn to go around the block the other way. One neighbor, Mr. Wetzel, got so mad he threatened to shoot Sudsy. We were quite sure he was joking, although his comment gave us pause!

Soon after meeting Barley's family, I could barely think or talk about anything else. My friends thought I was crazy – *you just get a dog or not, what's the big deal?* But I took the decision very, very seriously, ultimately deciding that I'd better not take on a two-month-old puppy.

As fate would have it, I received a call from Debbie, the breeder, several months later, in June of 1999. She had a seven-month-old male she was trying to place in a home. She thought of me. She had intended to show him, but I think he didn't quite grow into the specifications. His name was "JD", as in Jack Daniels, and his litter's theme was "Spirit". I drove to Peoria to meet JD with my friend Mitzi, who is known for her psychic predictions. JD pranced around, came up for pats and hugs, stared into the oven door, and played with a cat. She said, "That dog is for you. You have to get him."

I wasn't convinced. What would it be like to share my home after so many years alone? Would I be able to handle it? Would we get along? What if we tripped over each other? What would happen if it didn't work out? Despite my hesitation, Mitzi and I spent the drive home thinking of a new name for JD. He was no Jack Daniels. He was much too elegant and light-hearted. I always thought I wanted a dog named "Poncho" because the name implied comfort and warmth, something lacking in my life that I needed badly. But JD didn't look like a Poncho either. I couldn't see JD wearing an Indian blanket. We tossed around the possibility of Buddhist names such as Zen, and Nirvana.

A day later, without a dog name and in state of high anxiety, I called Debbie and said I wanted JD. During the next week, I ordered a kennel and some other supplies. But they hadn't come in yet when I drove to Peoria two weeks later. I'm surprised Debbie let me take the dog home. I showed up with no collar, no leash, although I did have a water bowl. It must have been obvious that I didn't have a clue. Debbie kindly put a slip collar around JD's neck, handed me a tiny lead, and bid us farewell. It broke my heart to tear JD from the comfort and love of his first family. He seemed as disoriented and scared as I felt.

We stopped in Casa Grande, Arizona to potty – the first time of many. To this day I don't have a dog door, and accompany Barley on most all of his evacuations. If I put him in the yard and I'm inside, he just stands at the sliding glass door and stares at me. He's more concerned with being together than doing his business.

JD's arrival in Tucson began the first, awkward stage of our relationship. I didn't have a name for him for several days, but called him "Puppy". I wanted him to have a name that was earthy and grounded so we would both feel nourished and settled. "Barley" emerged as just the right name. He was a complex carbohydrate. I was told the new name should rhyme with the old so it would be less confusing for him. Barley vaguely rhymed with JD, matched his coloring, was of the earth, and had the alcohol connection to his former name through beer. Spirit was clearly part of his essence. It worked, and we began our life together.

The first few nights and weeks were touch and go. Barley cried all night our first night together. I stayed up with him, hanging over my own bed to keep my hand on him through every breath. I wanted him to know he wasn't alone.

From the start, Barley simply refused to go in his kennel. I had no idea what he would do unattended, and he seemed to want to get into everything. I decided I would never be able to leave the house again, so I had a friend bring me groceries.

Several days later, realizing that I'd eventually have to go back to work, I broke down and called a woman who bred Golden Retrievers in Tucson and she came over for some private tutoring. We brought Barley to Pets Mart and picked out some supplies – treats, a bone, a good, rolled leather collar, a new leash. I watched her make a game of the kennel, throwing in treats, praising Barley profusely when he ran in to get them, letting him run in and out at will. She taught me the games and said to keep playing, always keeping the kennel door open. She'd be back the next day. The next day we filled a beef bone with peanut butter and he was allowed to chew on it only in his kennel. Then we graduated to shutting the kennel door briefly while he was immersed in his bone. Pam helped me for several days until Barley and I reached a more comfortable equilibrium. She strongly recommended that we attend school.

Barley has always been his own dog. We started taking a puppy class, and he ran through tubes and walked on different materials. One evening he got kicked out of class because he kept humping a lovely girl Golden Retriever. The teacher barked at me, "That is not appropriate or acceptable behavior!"

"No shit, Sherlock," I thought to myself as I slumped away from class with Barley pulling me like a maniac. I was clueless as to the solution. Barley and I went home to try and relax and reflect on our next steps.

We eventually graduated to the beginner's dog training class. It took months before I could let Barley within ten yards of the other dogs. All he wanted to do was play. I could barely hear the teacher's instructions from so far away. There were days I'd go home from class crying from the overstimulation of trying to control Barley amidst so many dogs and distractions. Until I discovered the secret of success: Cheese.

With cheese in my hand, Barley quickly moved up the ranks, successfully following instructions. Sit. Stay. Lay down. Heel. Hurry. Easy. Leave it. Right Turn. Left Turn. Barley, Come! We were by no means obedience stars but we forged a reasonable facsimile of attention and control. My friend Tony says that Barley would fly for the right treat.

After a few years of classes we decided the obedience thing was good enough. Barley loves doing tricks and performs like a champion. When it comes to taking walks, we have some push and pull. I find it fascinating to see how he attempts to reconcile both pleasing me and pleasing himself. Sometimes I want to keep walking and he wants to check out a cat, or see what's happening behind us. His first strategy is to plant himself in a standing position, regal and staring. When I get serious with my command he abruptly sits down to scratch his shoulder, usually turning 180 degrees. It's a sly move, as if to say, "I really would love to do what you want me to do, but I'm afraid that I have an itch."

He does two other things on walks that I have termed "precision sniffing" and "sniffing shenanigans." Precision sniffing involves getting on a sniff with the upper right corner of his right nostril, and it appears that he is sniffing up and down the trail of scent, molecule by molecule. My personal theory is that the level of focus and attention it takes to precision sniff is good for his brain and will prevent doggy dementia in his old age. I let him do it.

Sniffing shenanigans makes me want to scream. This is a much less focused kind of sniff. It appears that he isn't even concentrating on the smell at all, but rather looking for something else and pretending to sniff. Sniffing shenanigans often happens late at night on the coldest days in Tucson. He takes forever to find his spot. All that I want to do is get back inside.

About five years ago, as I was contentedly living day to day with Barley, I reconnected with Bob, the man I'm going to marry. Bob and I had dated eighteen years earlier when I lived in Salt Lake City, and he found me again by email five months before my dad died. One of Bob's early emails said "Vincent and I need to come down to Tucson and take you and Barley out on the town." Vincent is Bob's big orange cat. I knew then the relationship might have some potential.

During Bob's early visits to Tucson, Barley was the ice breaker. He provided fodder for conversation and a focal point when we felt awkward. I always come to life when I talk about and with Barley. He has turned a light on in me that I didn't know was there.

During one such visit the three of us walked to Himmel Park, a lovely tree-lined neighborhood park with a library and swimming pool. It was a moonlit night, and after quite a few months of contemplation, I was finally opening up to the possibility of romance. The three of us sat down on the side of the little hill facing west. I leaned back to look at the stars and gasped when I landed on something squishy --- fresh dog poop. My romantic musings fled, as did I, running home, cursing, with Bob and Barley trotting close behind.

My days with Barley are punctuated by daily walks, hikes, visits with friends, and trips to hardware stores. Barley has become the star of the neighborhood, receiving holiday gifts, and an open invitation to my architect neighbors' award-winning home and swimming pool. They say he's their favorite dog around. Neighbors stop their cars to say hello to my boy.

We've been through a lot together through the years. Barley was by my side as I grieved my dad's death, and as I struggled through helping my mom transition to assisted living. He has supported me with his happy, laid-back presence as I've wrestled with difficult sibling relationships and our arguments and issues that sometimes never seem to come to any resolution.

Barley and I survived eight years of the Bush Administration, and we rejoiced at the election of our first African American President, Barack Obama. We've been to peace rallies, friends' parties, and work events. Barley danced around with me in our living room when the Boston Red Sox finally won the World Series in 2004 --- a win that was especially poignant to my family because my dad just missed it. He died a few months too soon. He also just missed their previous win 85 years earlier in 1918 because he wasn't quite born yet. He must have watched every game in between.

The big events and little moments of my connection with Barley flow together in my consciousness. His before bed belly rub, and our "good morning" greetings are some of my favorite moments of every day. We like to be in the same room together most of the time. It's hard to say goodbye when I go to work. Barley is a touchstone to life for me and he is my beloved companion. We're both older and wiser and grayer than we were.

And now, Barley and I are preparing for the biggest, most uprooting change of our lives. At age fifty-one I'm planning to marry for the first time and at age ten Barley is preparing to have four cats as his step siblings. I admit I'm terrified and plagued with worries. Part of me would rather hold on to our little love nest, just as it is, always.

But if my life with Barley has taught me one thing, it is that although relationships aren't perfect, with attention and care they can and do work out, bringing unimaginable richness. Every time Barley pads over to me with his tail softly wagging, and looks up at me with his soulful brown eyes, he reminds me of the lesson I must carry close to my heart as we navigate the next phase of our life: It's all about love.

Post Script: My beloved Barley died at 11 ½ years old, before we had a chance to start our new life with Bob and the cats. He got very sick very quickly, and as best the doctors could tell it was either a burst aneurism or neurological disease. To say I am bereft doesn't touch the depth of pain I feel. Barley was the dog of a lifetime. He was my best friend and constant companion. I pray that time will heal some of the loneliness I feel without my Barley. And even though I know that nobody can replace Barley, I pray that the universe will bring me another dog who I can love and be loved by so completely. May he rest in peace and may we be in each other's hearts always.

Puppy Connection

by Maria Himers

In 1991 I spent a lot of time checking into breeders because I was looking for a very special Australian Shepherd puppy. There were a lot of phone calls, interviews; I had been searching for about a year-and-a-half. At the time I was a truck driver, spending many days at work over the road, and I needed to make sure this puppy would be happy with the kind of life I led, very active, but in the confined space of a truck cab for hours most days. So the selection process took time, but finally I found a kennel with dogs that would have the proper demeanor and the working ability I would need.

I was very excited when I was told they had a litter coming with the parents I had preferred, this made me very excited! The breeder and I had become good friends and I called weekly to say "hi," and make sure the mom was doing well. We had already discussed the special needs for this puppy, and concerns about potty training and she would keep the puppy a couple of extra weeks to enhance the learning and training needed. I was ready and really excited!

Then one night while I was sleeping I had this dream; it was so life like, I thought I was right there during the birth of a litter of puppies. I saw this very special puppy, and what I could see was a little face with a mask; it was very clear, just as if I was there. Then I woke up, and I could not get back to sleep, I was so excited, because now I knew which puppy would be mine. It would be the one with the little mask!

I had studied about puppies and training, and how to choose temperament early, the tests and how to do them, and what kind of temperament I needed, but after the dream, I knew it had to be the puppy with the mask.

I waited till after 9:00 in the morning, then I called the breeder. As soon as she answered I asked her if the puppies had been born. She was very happy, excited, and tired, because the puppies had been born in the middle of the night. I told her about the dream, and asked if one of the puppies had a mask. She took a few minutes to go take a careful look at the puppies, but there was not a mask on any of them.

I was so disappointed and just wrote it off as a strange dream.

I called a few days later and asked if I could see the puppies early to get the right puppy, and she told me that there had already been two puppies singled out for others, and to let her know when I would be in town next. The next week I got a load home, and we made an appointment to view the puppies. They would be 10 days old when I saw them. I so was excited to make the selection.

I made it home, spent the evening thinking and rethinking, hoping. I knew I would find the right puppy although I still felt strangely as if I needed that elusive puppy with a mask.

I got to the kennel a little early, but they were expecting me. The breeder started to bring the puppies out one by one; they were so cute, and their temperaments were all excellent! She kept asking me if I wanted to see the blue-eyed pups, but I was firmly against the blue eyes. I didn't want a dog for show, I wanted a working dog! Then finally we had gone through all the pups, they were all so cute and cuddly, tiny little things at 10 days old, but I didn't see "that pup," the one just for me.

I was thinking about taking second looks, or waiting for the next litter, so I asked again, are there any other pups? This time she told me "yes", there was one other pup, but she didn't want to show him because he was the runt of the litter and was so much smaller.

I insisted, partly because I knew a smaller dog would also work well in the truck. In fact, too large would be a problem!

She brought out the little pup; he was a little black "tri", which means he was black, with white and brown markings. As with all the other pups, there was no mask on him, something I realized that in some way I had still been hoping for. I was a bit heartbroken, but he had a wonderful temperament. He was barely the size of my hand, but he was just so sweet! I ended up talking to the breeder for quite a while, so long in fact that the little pup fell asleep. After about fifteen minutes he just rolled over in my hand, tummy up and stretched himself out, just like he was home!

I laughed, but didn't have the heart to wake him up, and when I showed the breeder what he had done, I told her, "He's made his mind up, so I guess I should too!"

Of course, that was the puppy I eventually took home, a dog who turned out to be so smart, wanted to please so much, but was tough enough to do whatever I needed him to do.

Over time I forgot all about wanting that puppy with a mask. I called my new dog Jake, and he went with me everywhere, always so good and so well behaved! Then it came time to finalize his registration paperwork. I had to take pictures for the AKC, but I didn't have a camera, so I got Jake ready and we went to a professional photographer.

It was a good shoot, but I never expected what happened when I got the photos back: in Jake's face shot you could clearly discern a mask! Even though I couldn't see his mask with my eye, all along I had had the pup of my dreams, my little guy with the mask!

Jake and I had a very happy and very long life together! We never lost that connection to one other, and he helped me daily doing whatever I needed him to do. In fact, this little runt of the litter saved my life on four separate occasions as well as saving my life every day of his life with his companionship and unquestioning love.

The Morrison Pack

by Christine Morrison

I count my blessings every day, beginning with my five dogs. I research training and nutrition and keep them exercised and healthy and in return they provide me with unconditional love and companionship. I am blessed to be able to *pay it forward* and combine two life passions: helping people and being with my dogs. Of my five-pack I have two certified pet assist therapy dogs who visit nursing homes, hospital wards and special needs classes on a regular basis. They are both members of the Happy Tails Pet Therapy organization in Georgia. HT animals visit facilities and participate in special events weekly.

When my husband brought Georgia Kaye, our Golden Retriever, home eleven years ago the shelter said she had been returned twice for 'behavior problems'. About three weeks after she arrived we found out *exactly* what that meant when she trashed our house from top to bottom! Georgia had a "thing" for plastic and we **had** a beautiful palm tree sitting in a plastic pot in our living room. Georgia somehow grabbed that recently-watered tree and chewed the pot to bits.

The end result was a mess of plastic pot, shredded tree and mud...up the walls, ground into the carpet and all over the stairs. Georgia left no stone unturned when it came to making that mess. Entering the house all I could say was "Oh My God"! I literally had **no** idea how to begin to clean it up, nor could I believe this had been masterminded by one sweet, adorable, "little" (sixty-five lbs), thirteen-month-old Golden Retriever. (I felt pretty certain this wasn't the work of our six lb. Yorkie or our Border Collie, who was doing her best to be invisible.)

Georgia, covered in mud, was hiding her shame under the table. My first thought was to crate her while I attempted to clean the mess, but she would have no part of that. The closer we got to the crate the more obstinate she became and all four legs went in different directions. I settled on having a long talk with her as punishment. Georgia **never** did another thing wrong from that point forward and went on to become a model therapy dog.

Since Georgia Kaye loves water, we joke that she is a $250,000 dog because we had to buy a house with a pool in the yard for her! When this girl was rescued her name was Georgia and we wanted to change it but it seemed to fit her personality so it stayed. Seven years later we moved to Georgia, so my husband now wishes her name had been Hawaii.

Our other therapy girl is Snoopy, aka Snoop Doggie Dog or the Snoopster, a six-year-old Lab/Corgi mix. Picture the head and body of a black Lab on the legs of a Corgi with a stub tail. Adopted as a puppy, Snoopy lived with a young couple for the first few years of her life. When the couple brought the new baby home, Snoopy, used to being a spoiled "only child," looked at the baby and snarled so off she went to a shelter. She was adopted again and for an unknown reason brought to animal control where she sat until a local rescuer saw the potential in her.

When I found her she was in boarding awaiting a foster home. so we became that foster. The first day we introduced Snoop to our pack she disappeared within a few minutes. After searching the bushes we realized she had jumped four feet vertically onto a rain barrel to get a drink! Needless to say, she loves agility. After watching her interact with our pack for a few weeks I evaluated her to see if she was therapy dog material. Eight weeks later she graduated and passed her Happy Tails test. Snoop's demeanor, and now perfect temperament, made her an excellent therapy dog.

As for the other three, we have a six-year-old Schnoodle; Sophie Ann, a six-year-old Shih Tzu; Toby Austin and a three-year-old Golden Retriever/German Shepherd; Cassiopeia Rae. We love all three of them dearly but they are all dysfunctional.

Toby came to us when he was thirteen months old; an owner surrender who had spent his life locked in a basement with his littermate, deprived of love and food. He receives an abundance of both now!

We are not sure what is wrong with Sophie Ann, but actually we think her brain may be wired wrong. Sophie has known nothing but love and affection for the five years she has lived with us and still she cannot trust. She is actually Georgia's dog and takes very good care of our aging Golden Girl. I think if anything ever happened to my husband and me Sophie would learn to hunt, shop and cook to keep Georgia happy!

Our last pack member, Cassie, is an absolutely gorgeous GR/GS mix who also came to us with trust issues and, like Sophie, has been unable to get past them.

My husband and I believe God put these dogs in our lives for a reason. I know in my heart of hearts that Sophie and Cassie, in particular, are in the right home.

I feel blessed to have two therapy dogs that put smiles on sick faces and help people be more at ease. Although they have had no specialized training, they instinctively know how to visit with each person. Snoopy has a favorite resident at a nursing home, so we visit her last. Snoop runs to her room, jumps up on her bed and smothers her with kisses. With all other residents she patiently enjoys the interaction.

As for Georgia, I am constantly amazed at her intuitiveness and the way she expresses unconditional love. During one special needs class visit, she was with a student when I asked her to come and visit another student. Georgia Kaye, always 100% obedient (after that first incident!), refused to move. I changed my tone and **ordered** her to come. She remained frozen. A few seconds later, the boy started seizing. I watched in amazement as she leaned into him to keep this little boy between her and his teacher.

Think that dog got an extra treat on the way home?!

During another school visit we were brought into a room with two students who had no verbal or motor skills. The students lay on the floor on separate blankets, their eyes following as I walked Georgia around them. She chose to lie down between their two blankets. Although neither child could speak, you could see joy in their eyes and the promise of a smile on their faces.

There are many silly stories I could share about my pack, and in particular my beautiful Golden Girl. After all, we've had eleven great years together and she has made twenty-two moves with us through four states! One time I picked her up from a grooming appointment and we went straight to bereavement camp for a pet therapy visit. If you have spent any time around seniors or kids you know they will tell it like it is, so I wanted to make sure she looked her best and smelled like a rose!

My team member and I arrived at the camp at the same time and let our dogs out. Bagel, the Beagle, jumped out of the car at the same time Georgia came bounding out of the truck. Unfortunately Georgia noticed something I wished she hadn't: a lake! Of course, she made a beeline for it, taking Bagel with her. The two of them enjoyed a nice swim while Bagel's owner and I stood on the banks of the lake screaming "get out of the water!" The kids had a good laugh over our two trained therapy dogs walking into the visit soaking wet and covered in mud!

I also help place dogs, finding the right matches. My brother, a Viet Nam vet, is a good example. He spent a couple of weeks with us shortly after we moved to Georgia. Charlie suffers from depression and had recently lost his wife and shortly thereafter, his dog. Of course my prescription to help ease his pain was another dog; the only creature on earth who can sense our emotions, predict our illnesses and ease our physical and emotional pain just by being close, yet ask nothing in return. We checked several rescues before finding a dog that needed him as much as he needed her. My brother returned home with sweet little Daisy, a terrier mix, cradled in his arms.

Dogs and helping people are my life passions. I am employed at a local college where I work with traditional and non-traditional students with disabilities. When not working, I volunteer, and oftentimes use my vacation time for pet therapy visits. The dogs in my life are my best friends, my constant companions and also my best emissaries out into the world; they bring love and peace wherever they go.

"The fidelity of a dog is a precious gift demanding no less binding moral responsibilities than the friendship of a human being."

– Konrad Lorenz, "Man Meets Dog"

Black Beauty

by Judy Taysom

Black Beauty performed double duty. An Australian Shepherd/Black Lab, she was seventy-five pounds and stood a little taller than knee level; soft fur, svelte. She was sweet as the day is long. Gentle. Happy. Trusting. Funny. Smart. Beautiful. Adorable. I was so proud to be her mama. She didn't care about my shortcomings.

Most people are familiar with PTSD as it relates to military personnel. I didn't serve in the military, but I trained my dog to be my PTSD buddy. I shocked my counselor when he told me I couldn't count on my dog to protect me, and I told him I didn't expect her to protect me. Protection was my job. Her job was to be my early warning system.

I loved walking with her and having people comment, "Great bodyguard." I'd laugh, but I'd never tell them she was a marshmallow. She let me know when someone was around so I could assess the situation. She picked up on my cues as to who was safe and who was not. She often stepped between me and other people, giving me the safe distance I needed. When anxiety kicked in I would sit on the floor petting her, and the anxiety would ebb.

She cared if I cried and attempted to comfort me. She let me know when my anger scared her. I hated scaring her, so I learned to control the anger. I learned commands didn't have to be barked at her because she understood a calm voice and requests. I used "please," "thank you," and "excuse me," with her. She responded to over ninety-four commands.

On days when I didn't want to face life, I did anyway because she needed to go outside. I exercised because she needed to go for a walk. People were interested in me because of Black Beauty, and she was a safe topic of conversation, an icebreaker. She loved me no matter how messed up I was.

When I knew she was nearing the end, I am ashamed to admit I was angry with her, especially the day before she died. I didn't want her to go. Yes, I was angry she was leaving me. I knew how difficult it would be with her gone.

I only pray she understood I was angry with me, not her, because I couldn't save her. I couldn't make her better. I couldn't make the pain go away. I couldn't make right all the things I'd done wrong. I couldn't fix anything. She was going where I couldn't follow.

She's been gone a few years now, and I miss her every day. But I don't regret those seventeen precious years in which she made me a better person. My dog really was my angel child.

For the Love of a Dog: an excerpt

by Patricia McConnell

In 1992, I fell in love with a dog named Luke. I brought him home from a herding dog trial in Minnesota one chilly, October evening, not sure if I'd keep him, not sure I wanted another dog. A gangly adolescent, Luke had been a disappointment to his first owner, who reported he wouldn't come when called and had failed his first herding lessons. I'd had my eye on him ever since he was a pup, and had told the owner to let me know if she ever decided to sell him. When he came up for sale I had more dogs than I needed, but every time I saw Luke something clicked inside, as if I'd finally found the combination to an old padlock I carried around, unopened. I took one last look at his bright, expectant face, wrote out a check, and drove him home through the red and orange hills of a midwestern autumn.

By sundown of the next day, Luke and I had fallen in love. I don't know any other way to describe it. I say "fallen in love" with the knowledge that eyes will roll, lips will purse and heads will shake. "That's pathetic," someone said to me once when I described my love for Luke. It seems that people either get it or not; like the yes-no simplicity of digital computers, the world sorts into people who've been deeply moved by a dog, or people who can take them or leave them. I learned to censor myself, to test the waters before volunteering some platitude like, "Yep, he's a great dog, Luke," instead of a deeper, more complex attempt to express how much I loved him.

I am buoyed by the knowledge that I am not alone. People come up to me at seminars, eyes full and bright with the beginnings of tears, and tell me they had a dog like Luke, "forever dogs" we call them, the canine loves of our life, dogs who expand our hearts and fill our souls in a way that nothing else ever had. Old Yeller was a book about a dog like that, a plain yellow dog who settled in the soul of a young country boy, and served as a cultural icon of the depth of devotion we can have for a dog.

No one describes the love between a person and a dog better than the late and eloquent writer, Caroline Knapp, in Pack of Two: The Intricate Bond Between People and Dogs. Speaking about the "remarkable, mysterious, often highly complicated dances that go on between individual dogs and their owners;" she said:

> That dance is about love. It's about attachment that's mutual and unambiguous and exceptionally private, and it's about a kind of connection that's virtually unknowable in human relationships because it's essentially wordless. It's not always a smooth and seamless dance, and it's not always easy or graceful—

love can be a conflicted, uncertain experience no matter what species it involves—but it is no less valid because one of the partners happens to move on four legs.

For twelve and a half years Luke and I danced together, sometimes so clear and so close to each other it was like moving as one, sometimes stumbling over each other's toes.

We were each other's soul mates, colleagues, family and best friends. I described him to everyone who would listen as my "one-in-million" dog and for reasons I don't understand, he seemed to love me as much as I loved him. [may have loved me, but no one-man dog] Luke was handsome and social, the one everyone wanted to sit next to at the dinner party, and he could schmooz with the best of them at banquets and cocktail parties. He was the perfect dinner guest who never neglected to thank the hostess, and could always be counted onto to flirt with the single woman in the corner. Flirt? Could someone possibly describe a dog as flirting? All I can say is that Luke adored everyone, but he loved women more than he did men, and always choose to sit beside one and charm her, head lolling like Stevie Wonder, his face open and full of happiness, one big paw in her lap.

My life was linked with Luke's in every way. Luke was the first thing I saw in the morning when he nosed my arm under the covers after the alarm went off, and the last thing I saw at night as I stroked his head on my way to sleep. Luke and I ran the farm together, he the trusty right hand man, me the landed gentry who knew the value of a smart, willing crew boss. It was Luke I turned to when flighty lambs needed loading, or when the ram jumped the fence to breed the ewes a month earlier than planned. It was Luke who leapt over a four-foot stall and saved me from a rampaging, horned ewe, and it was Luke who risked his life to stop a three-hundred pound ram from smashing me into pulp against a fence post.

Luke worked with me on dog-dog aggression cases with a kind of calm professionalism that I still find astounding. He put up with the insanity of taping 60 television shows in two months with grace and patience. He charmed audiences at seminars, speeches and book signings everywhere, and brought his black and white tuxedo of fur home to charge with abandon into mud and sheep poop to hold the ram off the feeder in the pouring rain. Luke loved being with me, herding sheep, playing ball, and running, running anywhere, after anything. He ran with the grace of a finely crafted sailboat coursing over deep water—no friction, no drumbeat of hooves on the soil—but with a smooth effortless glide that lifted my heart every time I watched it.

Luke was all of the above, but he wasn't perfect. He'd lose his temper on sheep, chase and even bite them when he was young, ears flat and eyes narrowed. He'd flash me looks better left untranslated when he didn't like my directions. I'm not perfect either, but just like soul mates everywhere, our flaws weren't enough to undermine the love we had for each other.

When Luke was middle-aged, I fell in love again, this time as if in slow-motion, with my human soul mate, Jim. After Luke's death, Jim admitted to a certain amount of jealousy between the two of them early in their relationship, although they eventually became great buddies. I called them "my guys," reveling in the feelings of warmth and fullness that comes with being loved. Jim, lucky me, is still here, but Luke died a year ago. His body is buried at the top of the farm road, where the hill pasture begins, where Luke would stand expectantly as I walked up the road behind him, waiting for me to catch up with him so he could play ball, or work sheep and run and run and run some more.

. . . .

There's a stone I had made for Luke at the top of the hill road, where the pasture opens wide and the setting sun highlights the words carved into its face. "That'll do, Luke, that'll do," it says. The words are said to working dogs all over the world when the chores are done and the flock is settled: "That'll do, dog; come home now, your work is done." Luke's work is done too. He took my heart and ran with it, and I hope he's running still, fast and strong, a piece of my heart bound up with his, forever.

-   Excerpted and reprinted from FOR THE LOVE OF A DOG: UNDERSTANDING EMOTION IN YOU AND YOUR BEST FRIEND by Patricia B. McConnell, copyright © 2005, 2006 by Patricia B. McConnell. Used by permission of Ballantine Books, an imprint of Random House, a division of Random House LLC.

Butterflies in the Rain

By Brandy Arnold

The shelter had named her "Beauty" and she most certainly was. The day I met her, she was crouched in the farthest end of her kennel at the shelter. How could someone abandon a dog so stunningly beautiful? The shelter didn't agree with her, she was terrified, trembling, trying to make herself as small as possible.

That's the one.

 All my plans of finding a small, short-haired dog flew swiftly out the window. I knew immediately, despite the fact that she wouldn't make eye contact, or greet me, and shirked away from my touch. I needed to save her.

She spent the entire ride home trembling on the floorboard of the car, cramming her 50-pound body into the tiny space designed for a pair of feet and not much else. I decided in that 15-minute ride home to rename her Molly. A song came through the radio at that exact moment, the most perfect possible moment of confirmation – Nirvana's *Kiss Molly's Lips*. And with that, I promised that I *would* kiss Molly's lips, every single day of the rest of her life. And I did. And she, mine.

The first few months of pet-parenthood were amazing – that very special kind of amazing you get when you bring a 6-month old, never-before-trained, teething puppy into your home. I replaced miles of baseboards after she graciously chewed them off the walls for me. I replaced wall-to-wall carpeting with wall-to-wall tile when she decided she loved the backyard far too much to potty there. At times it seemed as if she were thriving on a diet of shoes alone! I learned to sleep comfortably on a tiny sliver of my queen sized bed while Molly managed to spread her 50-lbs over the remainder.

I realized quickly that the most state-of-the-art sound machine couldn't compete with the soothing sounds of her gentle snore and that no medicine in the world could heal like her soft chin resting on my leg.

I've been fortunate enough to work from home for most of my career – aside from a few years in the corporate world where the absolute highlight of my life was the ecstatic, fur-flying, windmill-tail greeting I'd get from Molly at the end of each day.

While working at home one summer day, Molly was particularly persistent about going outside.

And coming right back in.

And going right back out.

And then coming right back in.

Normally in these moments, I'd just prop the back door open and give her free-reign. But on this August day in Florida, as my air conditioner struggled to keep the house a few degrees below sweltering, that wasn't an option. I let her outside, shut the door, and went back to work. Moments later I heard a frighteningly wicked bark from her that I'd never heard before. I ran outside in time to see the blur of a tall teenaged boy as he crested the top of the fence and darted through an adjacent yard.

About an hour later, a police officer came to the door and issued a summons. Molly had bitten the boy, right on the backside. It didn't matter to officers that he had been trespassing into my fenced-in yard. For two weeks, she was to remain indoors at all times, aside from the three times a day I could take her outside tethered to me by a 6-foot leash to go to the bathroom. She couldn't be walked, she couldn't bask in the sun, she couldn't chase squirrels. And, she had to be evaluated by an animal control officer who would determine if she was 'vicious.'

If it ever happens again, they told me, *she'll likely have to be put down.*

While the county punished her, I hugged her extra tight and thanked her for protecting me.

Just as Molly's house-arrest was coming to an end, that teenaged boy would be returning to jail for robbing another neighbor at knife-point.

Molly had appointed herself my protector. Of course, she was usually protecting me from squirrels. And in return, she only wanted love, belly rubs, and the occasional windows-down ride around town dribbling drool down the entire passenger side of my car.

Through 13 years of good times and bad, joy and sadness, milestones and speed bumps, illness and injury, it was Molly who was always by my side. Every morning began with the swipe of her black and pink dotted tongue across my cheek. Every night ended with her by my side, a part of her warm body touching me, if even just a paw stretched across the mattress to rest upon my ankle.

She had aged so gracefully, had never lost her vibrant spirit. When she started slowing down, sleeping in, hesitating to jump onto the bed at night, her joints arthritic from years of bounding down the stairs and leaping high into the air for a favorite stuffed toy, I would lie beside her, stroking those velvety ears with tears in my eyes at the mere thought of someday being without her, silently begging for more time.

Her seemingly perfect health and effervescent smile had kept the cancer growing inside of her a secret.

I lost my sweet Molly, my Molly Bear, my best good buddy, 1 year, 10 months, and 23 days ago. I wonder if I'll ever stop counting the time since she's been gone, the same way I counted her birthdays.

It was the one and only time I'd ever come home from the veterinarian's office without her. As I stood outside my front door, afraid to go inside, resisting the finality of it all, rain fell from the sky, mixing with the tears on my cheeks.

In times of intense sorrow, she was the one that always comforted me. How would I survive losing her, without her?

I made my way to the back porch and collapsed into a chair, looking out at her yard, where no less than a thousand of her chew bones were still buried. I was absolutely lost. That's when I spotted a Monarch butterfly, vivid and beautiful against the afternoon's dreary sky, fluttering about as if this were a warm, sunny day.

Butterflies don't fly in the rain.

As the days turned to weeks, then months, it seemed that butterfly was always around me. Whether I was alone at home, at a park with friends, or sipping coffee at an outdoor café, there she was. In times of intense pain or sorrow, extreme happiness or joy, I'd always secretly give a quick glance around to find her. She was always there, even as Spring rains became Summer heat waves, and as Fall leaves finally fell to the ground in the icy cold of Winter.

When the quietness of Molly's absence was too deafening and the emptiness too heavy to bear, I decided it was time to find another dog, to once again fill my life with love and laughter and drool and fur.

I struggled with the decision. Was it too soon? Would it be a disservice to Molly? Would I secretly wish the new dog was her? Could I possibly love another dog as much?

I'd always found comfort in running my fingers through Molly's long, thick fur. It was my only criteria for a new furry friend. The butterfly danced around me as I nervously made the call to adopt a young Golden Retriever from a few towns over. As I made the hour and a half drive, I hoped I was doing the right thing, that the butterfly's appearance was my "sign" that it was ok, but began to doubt myself as I got closer to the house where I would be picking her up.

When I finally arrived and anxiously approached the front door, there it was - my butterfly. One hundred and four miles away from home, she was dancing around in the nighttime sky.

Butterflies don't fly at night.

"An animal's eyes have the power to speak a great language."

- Martin Buber

King of Sadness

by Lon "Veteran Traveler" Hodge

My wife calls me the King of Sadness. She won't read anything I write if she is not in a place where she can safely cry. While she sees the need for me to be cathartic and to give others permission to grieve the losses in their life by being honest about my own, she begs me to write more stories of joy and celebration. I think I do. Let me explain…

Today in the lobby of the hotel where we stay while I am receiving care at the VA, a long-term resident overheard me imploring the desk clerk and manager to look out the back door. There, autumn had gently pushed aside summer, the temperature was a perfect 65 degrees and the sun was burning away a sweet fog that had been gently communing with the pond around which Gander walks every morning.

The resident, who for as long as I have known him, has been full of anger and is known for being disgruntled and volatile and feared as mentally unstable. He has more than one sadly descriptive nickname. We parted ways after he once reached down in an attempt to strike Gander when he thought Gander might brush against him. He hates dogs and has fabricated stories to management in an attempt to get them banned from the hotel. If I thought he could be trusted with an animal, I think there is no human more in desperate need of a pet than this man.

Another guest asked our hotel curmudgeon today what everyone was going to look at outside. His reply: "Nothing. Just some fog on the pond." His disconnection from the beauty, only a few steps away, refreshed in me an understanding of things I had desperately needed to comprehend.

That "little fog" today, surrendered itself to a beautiful day, and took with it some of the pain and confusion I had been feeling. At the BMW Golf Championships yesterday, Gander and I were both emotionally and physically bruised when a crush of people eager to get an autograph from Tiger Woods pinned us against a retention fence. We were collecting the autographs on a flag to donate to Freedom Service Dogs to auction at their fund raiser this coming weekend. Tiger, afraid of the consequences of staying much longer, stopped signing one person short of our position which we had staked out for almost two hours. We left the course almost immediately.

On the way home I thought through my day. A few hours earlier, another golf star's press agent had responded to my request to take a pic of him and Gander for an upcoming article about the PGA and wounded warriors by saying that the pro felt if he couldn't take pictures with all vets he would take pictures with no vets. I was licking my pride-induced wounds when I heard the news of a mass shooting in Washington. I quickly wrote a Facebook update: "The more I am around people, the more I love my dog." My wife reported to me today that I kept her awake as I fought the demons of the day through a fitful night.

There was a book on the market several years ago entitled, The One Minute Meditator. At first glance you might react cynically and believe it to be a cheap pop culture attempt at mindfulness. Not so. In a country where TV news hopes to consume the better parts of our day with polarizing and demoralizing information; where we have lowered our heads six inches, below where it could be in appreciation of the beauty around us, in order to search for "likes" or another SMS; where a golf pro who makes more in a week than my father, a decorated hero who gave his life for his country, made in a lifetime cut short by war, hasn't time for a picture; where I have seen my government lower the flags to half-mast more in the last 13 years to honor those lost to mass murder than I saw it lowered the whole of the rest of my life in celebration of those who served us, it is important for us to start finding the pleasure in simple acts.

We would do well to drop what we are doing for a moment of silence, or to savor the taste of something delicious in our mouths, or to close our eyes for sixty seconds and let music translate the words our hearts desperately want everyone to understand, to watch a sunrise, or to stroke the fur of an appreciative pet.

How many suicides could be averted? How many could we lift out of depression? How many innocent souls could remain here on earth instead of being violently sent early on their journey to whatever awaits us beyond this life? To how many could we give a moment of pleasure before they are caught up again in the din and roar of a hurried, harried day of trivial pursuits we have come to believe are important?

This year I have watched closely as Gander created thousands of those kinds of meditative minutes. He was a conduit to all that is good in the here and now and to everything in need of remembering. He has provided a spiritual firewire, for me and hundreds of others he has not even met, needed to access the divine. He has facilitated smiles and goodwill in people worldwide. He has started the healing of many a broken spirit.

How he has nurtured health in me and others is important: Often it starts with a memory and a moment of shared grief or loss. He reminds us of the dog that made their lives whole and the times and people that surrounded that period; he joins people with memories of a better time by taking them back to that place before somehow guiding them into the present and a celebration of what once was, maybe with the wag of a tail or an understanding kiss on the hand or cheek. Saul Bellow said, "Everybody needs his memories. They keep the wolf of insignificance from the door." We remember a time when we felt wanted, needed and important.

Grief and the sadness that goes with it are part and parcel of appreciating all that is good. They are travel companions much more comfortable with each other than we know. I have long thought that monsters willing to strike an innocent animal or discharge a lethal bullet in the direction of a stranger must have a monstrous sorrow so tightly constrained that there is little room in their hearts for anything but anger or rage.

I may well be the King of Sadness with Gander as my advisor: A Merlinesque wizard who can summon the past and cast a spell that empties us of sorrow so we might appreciate, if only for a minute, the joys around us that never really left. I just provide food and shelter for this magical character. He makes us wise by example and allows us to sleep better at night, to be better to all creatures we will meet in our short lives. He helps stretch those meditative minutes into hours, days, weeks..... . I'll sleep better tonight.

Afterword

by LBH

"You never know the hurt others endure in this world behind the closed windows of their life, or the joy a simple act of kindness can bring."

—Jennifer Skiff

This book, in its abbreviated electronic format, has generated letters from around the globe and has grown Gander's community on Facebook and Twitter of like minds and supportive hearts. It has become a safe port in the turbulent waters of this new sea of information. It is a place where commercialism, politics, ego and negativity just don't feel at home. It is a place where shared experiences are valued and encouraged.

If an experience is true it can act, in the retelling, like an emotional tuning fork and will resonate feelings deep inside of us. Each of these stories, complete as they can be, are shorthand for our own stories. They help us recall moments of love, loss, inspiration or renewal that help us better understand our relationships with our friends, families and four-legged companions. There is not a day that passes that I am not moved to tears or burst into laughter because of an email or a message from one of Gander's friends.

"I recently purchased "In Dogs We Trust" and read the entire book in less than 2 days. It was one of those books that I couldn't wait to read as soon as I heard about it months ago. I probably should have waited a bit before reading the book as it had me in tears the entire time. However, I did save "The Voices at

Arlington" for last and am so very thankful for not only the book but for your contribution. On September 29th I lost my baby brother Sgt. Jesse Valerio, a 10 year active member of the Army. He did a tour in Afghanistan and two tours in Iraq as a combat medic. He quietly suffered from sever PTSD which resulted in death by suicide. As his big sister, I am having an extremely hard time dealing with this loss. Your short story was like a balm for my wounded soul. It didn't make the pain go away but it definitely made it bearable. On Tuesday Oct 22nd we say our farewells to my brother in Arlington as he's laid to rest. Knowing that you and Gander may someday come across his final resting place has brought me some measure of peace. Thank you so very much for this wonderful book. You have touched a life in a way that cannot be expressed by words.

A New Gold Star Family Member"

My original goal this year was to bring about a greater awareness of PTSD and offer dogs, not drugs, as one alternative to the horrors of the anxiety caused by trauma. Public discourse about suicide and invisible wounds are still conversational IEDs, but I have seen many people find the courage to voice their fears and look for solutions other than suicide because they now know they are not alone. This book has created good, in more ways than I could ever have dreamed.

We don't speak loudly enough about suicide because we are afraid that weakness may have been a factor in someone's choice to die rather than fight an ocean of fear with a useless weapon. And we worry about that part of ourselves that one day might answer our own panic, depression or chronic pain with an overdose or a bullet.

We have knowledge of PTSD, but don't yet recognize the pandemic, insidious presence of PTSD because we think they might just be malingerers drawing benefits for wounds they do not have, or sexual trauma victims who somehow invited trouble. So, we end up devaluing those who end their days exhausted after trying to give the appearance of normalcy while they are so terrified by everyday events they can barely breath–those who, if they dared, would scream for help. And many other suffer night terrors and daily panic, but won't admit to it for fear of being thought of as mentally defective, weak, or dangerous.

Some people have written to me that reading about what dogs have done to save the lives of people like me, has enriched their lives and given them a positive charge that enables them to face another day of chemotherapy, loneliness or chronic illness. And others are simply grateful for a space that remains uplifting.

Gander no longer belongs to me. He is a global citizen. He is listed on the cover of this book not as a novelty. He is the reason most of these writers have come together. If I drew a tree, all but one or two branches would lead back to him. Though I regard

Gander as special, his greatest gift to me is the same one given by dogs to every writer in this book: unconditional love and forgiveness. What other being, beyond an angel or bodhisattva, could so easily forgive your human trespasses and then kiss away your tears of guilt and shame? Albert Schweitzer said, "Until he extends the circle of his compassion to all living things, man will not himself find peace." I am guessing his old dog, Turck, had a hand in that aphorism.

To all of you whose monumental kindness so generously supported my incredible journey toward health and the making of this modest book: Thank you. From the bottom of my heart, thank you.

There is so much more to come.

Thank You

There are hundreds of people to thank. These are the people who gave time, talent and money to make this book happen, plus a list of supporters of the Indiegogo campaign that got this project off the ground. There are many debts here I can never repay.

Of course, I have to thank my wife, Xiaoli, for her unwavering faith and love and for being there through the worst of times. She always believes the nightmares will subside.

In no particular order, from the bottom of my heart, I am grateful:

Lynn Bukowski, Briana Ore, Sharyl Norman, Brooke Arnold, Xu Xiaoli, Brandy Arnold, Katherine Clark, Jamie Downey, Larry Rubly, Patricia McConnell, Missy Pietrowiak, Lourdes Sosa, Summer Lynn Glasgow, Jane Morris Procacci, Sergeant John Nolan, Stacey Candella, Bishop Hinners, Diane Carbo, Franklin Thomas, SEAL of Honor, Rob Dubois, Aimee Lynn Dee Culler, Susan Hess, Nicole Stokes, Jerome Evenson, Pamala Englehart, Cyrilla Baer, Kevin Hanrahan, Haus of Paws, Kerry O'Connor, Jeannie Murphy O'Connor, John Atterberry. Dr. Paige Lasson, Mark Racas, Jillian Webb, Alexandra Thurman, Mary Ann Helpern, Thérése Weiner, Geoff Lason, Anthony Bennie, Brian Nordman, Jim Poland, Dogington Post, Keir Willett, Garvey Harris, Patty Harris, David Bolinsky, the crew at Caribou Coffee in Libertyville and Lake Forest, Illinois and all the authors in this edition and the next!

--Lon & Gander

Contributors

A former EOD trained ordnance officer, professor and Veteran Traveler blogger **Lon Hodge** is also an award winning poet, writer and now activist for suicide prevention among fellow Veterans and victims of trauma. He was one of the early pioneers in social media as a member of Task Force Delta at the Army War College. He travels with his PTSD service dog Gander in support of awareness of the healing power of dogs. He is on the board of directors of numerous charities and donates time and talent as health allows.

Marie Anton was a poet and writer who spent part of her small Social Security income every month supporting various animal causes. She never met a dog she didn't love. She died in 2007 and stipulated in her will that a part of her moderate estate go to rescue organizations.

Robert W. Hill has published poems in such magazines as *Minnesota Review, Southern Review, Shenandoah, Southern Poetry Review, Ascent, Red Clay Reader, Atlanta Review, Arlington Quarterly* and *Cold Mountain Review.* With the late Richard J. Calhoun, he co-authored *James Dickey* (Twayne, 1983), and co-edited *South Carolina Review* (1973-85). He is currently Professor, Emeritus, at Kennesaw State University and Adjunct Professor of English at Marshall University

Ian Hubbard, age 10, is a 6th grade student. He is a voracious reader and an accomplished actor. He loves dogs. Corky the Corgi was adopted from Wayside Waifs, a no-kill shelter in Kansas City, Missouri that houses up to 800 animals at a time and places approximately 5,400 animals with new families each year. A few months after Corky died, Ian and his family returned to Wayside Waifs and adopted a Black Mouth Cur puppy they named Arlo Jedediah Finch Hubbard.

Jim Poland is a steadfast advocate for veterans having grown up on U.S. Air Force bases around the world. He spends his days helping people and organizations achieve more of what they want; more results, more joy. Most days, he posts tweets at @JimPolandcom. Jim lives in York, Pennsylvania with his dear wife, Julie, and his precious daughters, Lauren and Allison. The family is blessed with the companionship and joy of two dogs, Cookie and Boomer, the lap warming of their all-black cat, Coal, and the sparkly Miss Fishy. When Jim isn't taking hikes with his pups and Julie, he's watching his daughters zooming down the pool at swim meets or scoring goals at water polo and lacrosse, and watching and listening to them play their flute, clarinet, saxophone, and piano.

Kevin Hanrahan is the author of the novel-in-manuscript, *Paws on the Ground*, about U.S. Soldiers and the dogs that protect them in the treacherous terrain of Afghanistan. He is the winner of the 2011 James River Writers Conference "Pitchapalooza" competition. The novel is based on Hanrahan's twenty years of Army service, and his experiences as a company commander in Iraq and as the Deputy Provost Marshal for U.S. forces in Afghanistan. While in Afghanistan, Hanrahan spearheaded the surge of dogs into Afghanistan and lobbied the Army to adopt an innovative and life saving explosives detecting dog program.

Lynnette Bukowski is the Founder/Director of LZ-Grace (Landing Zone Grace) Veterans Retreat, a freelance author and artist, the mother of three, the therapeutic foster mother of 15 (now all grown) and a recent widow of a 32 year veteran Navy SEAL (Sidow). She is now all of the ages she has ever been and continues to grow her soul, mind, body and spirit by full immersion in life.

Stephanie Weaver is an experience consultant, speaker coach, recipe developer, and food photographer. She finds inspiration and delight as an occasional yogi, urban farmer, and puppy wrangler. She lives in San Diego with her husband Bob and their Golden retriever Daisy. She has authored *Golden Angels: A Pet Loss Memoir*, *Creating Great Visitor Experiences,* and the *Twelve Terrific* series of recipe collections. Find her on the web as her alter ego The Recipe Renovator, creating ridiculously yummy, gluten-free recipes made from plants.

Lynn Rasmussen, is a married professional woman whose life was impacted by dogs; specifically, Molly, her German Shepherd. She has been passionately involved with the Delta Society Pet Partners Therapy Dog Team.

Best-selling author **Bruce Littlefield** has been deemed a "lifestyle authority" by the NY Times and "modern day Erma Bombeck" by NPR. He is the author of numerous books including one he and his rescue Westminster wrote, entitled *The Bedtime Book for Dogs*, which is the first book that dogs understand. Originally from South Carolina, Bruce has designed and owned two award-winning restaurants, and Edgewater Farm, his 1940's Catskills farmhouse, which he renovated and decorated himself, has been featured in numerous publications. His latest book is *Moving In: Tales of an Unlicensed Marriage* and includes many adventures with his food hound Jasper.

Joanna Perry-Folino is a full time theatre and film professor at a community college in California. She currently resides in Burbank where she writes and produces narrative and documentary films and stage plays. She is currently working on a novel, "Ian Down Under" about her adventures in Australia and America discovering her roots, as well as writing a one-woman show. She believes strongly in the power of community to empower both men and women throughout the world. And she loves dogs, women's best friend. Certainly hers.

In the spring of 1991 **Jit Bahadur** joined Himalaya Rescue Dog Training Center Sundarijal at first as a volunteer mountain guide to learn the art of Search and Rescue (SAR) dog care and training. Over the years, Jit was a SAR team leader on many parties for lost travelers such as the well-documented search for lost Australian trekker James Scott, lost child Sebastian Bergerhoff, Swedish trekker Tim Alven, and many more. The piece excerpted here is from his memoir-in-progress, Vanished in Nepal.

Alan Paul is the author of One Way Out: The Inside History of the Allman Brothers Band and Big in China: My Unlikely Adventures Raising a Family, Playing the Blues, and Becoming a Star in Beijing, which is currently being developed as a film by Ivan Reitman's Montecito Pictures. While living in China Alan authored an award winning column for the Wall Street Journal. Alan, his wife Rebecca, and their three children now reside in Maplewood, NJ. His blog can be found at www.alanpaul.net.

Julie Poland, author of Changing Results By Changing Behavior, is a certified business coach and facilitator for people and companies who want to achieve more. She founded Summit HRD 23 years ago to help individuals build upon their strengths and thereby build greater awareness, purpose, competence, well-being, and best of all – results. Julie posts on TheSummitBlog and at @JuliePoland most business days. She lives in York, Pennsylvania with her husband, Jim, their daughters, Lauren and Allison, two beloved dogs, Cookie, whose story she relates in this book, and Boomerang, their cat Coal, and a fish.

After twelve years of active duty as a U.S. Navy SEAL, **Mike Ritland** started his own company, Trikos International. Along with training dogs for the SEAL Teams, he continues to supply working and protection dogs to a host of clients, including Department of Homeland Security, U.S. Customs, Border Patrol, TSA and the Department of Defense. He has trained hundreds of working dogs, and has over 15 years of experience in importing, breeding, and raising multiple breeds of working dogs. He founded the Warrior Dog Foundation to help retired Special Operations dogs live long and happy lives after their service. Proceeds from his NY Times best-seller, Trident K9 Warriors, are donated to the Warrior Dog Foundation.

George White is a former sergeant in the U.S. Marine Corps and network sitcom writer, now battling it out on the blogosphere. A proud sixth-generation Texan and polo-playing enthusiast who lives on both coasts, he finds life lessons and great wisdom in the food he eats. He's still waiting for "his" dog.

National Mill Dog Rescue was established in February 2007, in honor of a forgiving little Italian Greyhound named Lily. Theresa Strader, NMDRs Founder and Executive Director, rescued Lily from a dog auction in Missouri. Prior to that day, Lily had spent the first seven years of her life as a commercial breeding dog. Determined that her years of misery would not be in vain, Strader started NMDR, giving a voice to mill dogs across the country and rescuing over 8,000 dogs to date. **Pam Horton**, who adopted her new best friend Olive from NMDR, lives in Colorado Springs with her husband, 2 children, four dogs and one cat. She is now a volunteer at National Mill Dog Rescue. **Kelly Thompson**, mom of Izzy, is founder of Faerie Tale IG Rescue/Rehab/Rehoming located in Alberta, Canada.

Sharyl Norman is a petroleum engineer who has worked in the oil fields of Wyoming for thirty-five years. She is also a rancher whose passion is her horses, dogs and cats. She uses Equine Facilitated Learning Coaching to help people work out their life issues, and is planning to expand her practice to helping Veterans with PTSD.

Susan Herbert, Lone Star "Dog Whisperer", is always delighted for an opportunity to spread the word about the almost magical process of repairing people-pet relationships and stopping the insanity in households that have "gone to the dogs." A certified Level 3 Canine Specialist of America's Canine Academy, Susan transforms the lives of desperate pet owners whose adorable Christmas puppies have mysteriously turned into hounds from HELL. **Mark German**, America's Canine Expert, has a special gift. Simply put, he changes people's lives. Utilizing his advanced knowledge of canine psychology and behavior, Mark travels the United States helping people save the "bad dogs" that other experts have either given up on, or lack the knowledge to help the dog through conventional means. He has saved thousands of aggressive, fearful, and "death row" dogs.

Anthony Bennie is Founder and President of Clear Conscience Pet. He has devoted over twenty years to the natural pet nutrition industry. He started Clear Conscience Pet in 2010 with his wife, Amanda Malone Bennie, a natural pet retailing pioneer and expert in her own right. The company's mission is to create innovative, healthy, and sustainably sourced nutrition for dogs and cats. Anthony has been published extensively in national and regional consumer and trade print media with articles on all aspects of pet nutrition and the pet care industry.

Cheryl Arnold Moseley, RN, photographer, and public speaker, is currently writing her memoirs which will be announced on her website, www.eyeoftheworld.us. Having traveled around the globe several times, she volunteered in nursing and health education in Afghanistan and Himalayan villages since 1972, participated in several high altitude mountain climbing expeditions, studied with the Dalai Lama, and nursed the sick and dying along side of Mother Theresa. For the past twenty years, Cheryl worked as an RN Surgical assistant with her husband, a neurosurgeon. Another passion she supports is the Arnold Endowment for the Visually Impaired in honor of her parents.

Jane Procacci, originally from Charleston, SC, now resides in Garner, NC with her husband, three cats, one bird and of course, Liesel. Jane grew up in Apex, NC where her parents owned and operated a boarding kennel, which is still in operation today. Jane often volunteers her time to rescue groups, local and nationwide. She also volunteers her time online with individuals diagnosed with Interstitial Cystitis (IC) who are needing support

Paul Owens, the original Dog Whisperer, is the author of several books including the best selling *The Dog Whisperer: A Compassionate Nonviolent Approach to Dog Training*, which has sold over 300,000 copies all over the world. He also produced and is featured on the Dog Whisperer DVDs, Volumes One and Two. Paul began training dogs in 1972. He is a member of the Association of Professional Dog Trainers and a leading proponent of positive, nonviolent animal training in the United States. His programs are unique in that stress management methods for humans are presented as part of the classes. Paul is the director of the Raise with Praise Teacher Training Program, and the founder/director of the children's after-school, violence prevention program, Paws for Peace.

LinnieSarah Helpern is a blogger, editor, and journalist focusing on popular culture and cinema. She attended UNCW, Dartmouth, and Charlotte School of Law, all of which added up to a lot of degrees but not a lot of job prospects, so... she writes! You can read some of her work at thehorrorhoneys.com. She currently lives in Los Angeles, California and spends most of her time at work daydreaming about her big fluffy mutt, Eliot.

Holly Altman is the Director of Alumni Affairs for the University of Arizona College of Medicine. She has found her true calling in program development and leadership. One of her greatest joys is leading programs that create positive change to expansive success.

Born and raised on a dairy farm in Illinois, **Marla Himers** is a Disabled Air Force Veteran with PTSD and a precious Australian Shepherd, Bishop, as her Service Dog. Hobbies include hiking, photography, and reading. She spends a great deal of her time supporting Veterans and the benefits of Service Dogs.

Christine Morrison is a vegetarian with a passion for animals and helping people. Driven by her passion she has worked most of her life in the non-profit sector for companies like the Kent Waldrip National Paralysis Foundation and the Susan G. Komen Breast Cancer Foundation. She now works with disabled traditional and non-traditional students at a local college. When not working, she spends her time with her husband and five furkids or volunteering to help people or for animal causes.

Judy Taysom grew up in Arizona, and writes Christian Romance novels under the pen name Laurel Hawkes.

Patricia McConnell is an ethologist, author, advice columnist, radio host, certified applied animal behaviorist, and dog trainer. She holds a PhD in zoology from the University of Wisconsin-Madison. Most of her work centers on the evaluation and treatment of behavioral problems in dogs. She received the honor of "Writer of the Year" from the International Positive Dog Training Association. She is the author of *The Other End of the Leash*, and *For the Love of a Dog*.

Brandy Arnold is editor and contributing writer at DogingtonPost.com, the internet newspaper all about dogs. Through a deep, life-long love of dogs, Brandy has learned patience, experienced unconditional love, been alerted to every squirrel within a block radius of the house, and ingested enough dog hair to knit several sweaters! She dedicates her time and talent to improving the lives of all dogs through advocating, educating, and inspiring others.

Join our adventures at

http://facebook.com/ganderservicedog

and

http://veterantraveler.com

and

In Dogs We Trust on Twitter at **@VeteranTraveler**